WORTH IT

WORTH IT

OVERCOME YOUR FEARS
AND EMBRACE THE LIFE
YOU WERE MADE FOR

BRIT BARRON

 Broadleaf Books

Minneapolis

WORTH IT
Overcome Your Fears and Embrace the Life You Were Made For

Cover image: Jorge Macias
Cover design: Sami Lane

Print ISBN: 978-1-5064-6327-8
eBook ISBN: 978-1-5064-6328-5

To my sweet Sami: thank you for being the mirror I needed to truly see myself and to see what is good and pure and true.

To our parents and those family and friends who chose to walk this journey with us: thank you for choosing growth over comfort, freedom over fear, and love over everything else. Without you, we would not have come this far.

CONTENTS

FOREWORD

The first time I ever saw Beans (yes, Brit Barron *is* the author of this book, but most of us refer to her as Beans—don't worry, you will too by the end of the read), she was preaching. I learned some important things about her that day at church, which I feel duty-bound to share with you now.

First of all, Beans is a ridiculously talented communicator. She has this skill of taking topics that seem nearly impossible to understand and breaking them down in a way that anyone can grasp. She's funny and thoughtful and wise and you don't need to take my word for it—just keep reading and you'll get it just like I did on that sunny summer Sunday all those years ago.

The second thing you need to know about Beans is that once you interact with her (even just through the pages of this book) you *will* want to be real-life best friends with her. I know this is true because on that day years ago the first thing I thought was, "Wow, this girl is so cool!" That thought was followed almost immediately by a desire be awesome enough to be friends with the cool girl. For real. Beans brings out the aspiring middle schooler in nearly every woman she meets. Yet, as confident and effortlessly fly as she is, she never once makes you feel like you're an outsider even if she just met you eleven seconds ago.

I walked over to her after church that day and introduced myself, and it hasn't struck me until just this moment how utterly unlikely it is that she and I would eventually become the dearest of friends. I'm a mother of four with extensions on my nails, hair, and lashes. She rocks Vans and T-shirts and the last time she wore makeup (just a little lipstick) she did it as a joke and still spent the rest of the day worried that she looked "too intense." I am a hardcore enneagram number three (that means "achiever" if you don't speak enneagram) who can barely look at any situation without trying to attach a goal to it and fight for traction. Beans is an enthusiastic seven who finds positivity in literally every situation and who told me once: *"I want to make just enough money to survive so I can spend the rest of my time hanging out with Sami—"*

That statement still haunts me to this day.

I really like making out with my husband Dave. Beans spent the first two years of our friendship talking about her "really good girl friend Sami." She is African American and Mexican American and I'm a white girl from hillbilly stock. We are extremely different people on the surface but we're utterly in tune with our values. The core values of our friendship circle include but are not limited to: Beyoncé, happy hour, group tattoos, the power of a good hat, the power of a good meal, showing up authentically, vacations, and a really, really intense devotion to vision-casting our futures in beautiful locations.

No, I am not making that last one up—it's a *real* thing.

I've learned over time that it doesn't matter how unlike two people are; if you hold core beliefs sacred you can always build a beautiful relationship. One of the greatest shared beliefs in our circle of friends (beyond Moscow mules at happy hour) is simply this: You are enough *as you are.* You are worthy. You are worth the effort. You are worth fighting for!

And so we're clear, I don't mean that you're worth a partner fighting for you romantically (though that's certainly true and a dreamy thought). In this instance I'm not talking about your worth in relation to anyone else. I mean that *you*, the real you, deserve to live your truth, even if it means pushing yourself out of your comfort zone. Beans will talk about that a lot in the coming pages, and while I know she'll tell you this truth I want you to hear it from me, her friend, so you know that it's true: Beans becoming who she is *cost her.*

There was a price to her truth.

It cost her jobs, her church, her community, her safety, and her security, and revealed the sad reality that some people who claim to love you the most only deal in conditional love.

When Beans tells you that it's hard live your freedom, believe her.

When she tells you that it's worth it—that you're worth it—believe that too.

Recently at one of our RISE conferences (of which Beans has been my partner in crime since the beginning) a young woman came up to me in the picture line.

"I have a secret," she blurted out. "It's something I've never said to anyone but I saw Beans speak today and you keep saying we should be ourselves and I just want someone to know. Can I tell you my secret?" She was giddy and nervous and believe it or not, I get this kind of thing a lot. "Of course," I told her.

She took a deep breath and looked me in the eye.

"I'm . . ." She let it draw out for a few seconds as if finding the courage to leap. "I'm totally gay." She finished the rest in a rush so fast I could hardly make out the words. "And I'm going to go home and I'm going to tell my family and it's fine, right Rach? I mean, my family definitely won't disown me, right? And it will be okay and my whole world won't crumble, right?"

I'll tell you what I told that sweet young woman that day. The truth is, I don't know if it will be all right. I don't know how your family or your friends or your community will react to your honesty. Living authentically is not for the faint of heart.

The truth is, you might be attacked when you stop apologizing for who you are, be it a queer college student, or an ambitious mama, or an affirming pastor, or a person of color fighting through the injustice of a broken system. You might be attacked because your freedom will remind others that they're still in chains. But a life lived only in pursuit of other people's approval is a life wasted.

Don't back down.

I don't believe it will be easy to claim who you are, but I know it will be worth it.

xo, Rach

—Rachel Hollis, author of *Girl, Wash Your Face* and *Girl, Stop Apologizing*

INTRODUCTION: CHOOSING SPRING

For the first thirty-two years of my life, I never experienced what a sunburn felt like. The magic of melanin makes it possible for black people to consistently evade this sun-based pain, but a few years ago, I really pushed the limits too far. One of my best friends from college is the kind of person whose birthday requires extravagance every year (she's wonderful in that way), so for this particular birthday, we took a red-eye from Los Angeles to Miami. We planned to spend two whirlwind days dancing our hearts out and relaxing on the beach. But you know the problem with a red-eye? You land *hours* before you can check into your hotel.

When we arrived at around nine o'clock in the morning, we went straight to the beach and fell asleep for the next four hours. It was not a cute nap on the beach. I am positive that people walking by thought we had all been shot with tranquilizer darts. I was lying flat on my stomach in the sand and did not move for four hours. That was *a lot* of Miami sun shining directly on my back. Later that night, I began experiencing a new and unusual pain. My back hurt. But it wasn't like muscle pain but like my entire back was tender to the touch. Everything it touched made it sting, and it was radiating heat. What the hell was this torture! One of the other girls on the trip was experiencing the symptoms. (This trip was 100 percent black girls, so there were no sunburn experts in the group.) At first I wondered how I could have caught what I imagined was a rare disease that only she and I had. Was it a rash? Did I get bit by a radioactive bug at the beach? How long would I feel like this? Was it permanent?

I was baffled by my condition. Not long after my symptoms set in, I called my wife—not only because wanted to talk to her but also because now that I had this mystery back condition, I just wanted her to know I loved her if the worst should happen. To set the scene for you, we had recently done the DNA test where you spit in the tube and it tells you where you are from. My wife's came back as 99.6 percent Irish and British. Needless to say, she has had her fair share of sunburns. On more than one occasion, she has gotten sunburned just driving in the car on a sunny day. But here's the thing—her skin turns instantly red, which makes it easy to tell when she's burned. We were sunburned but couldn't tell by looking at it. I was on the phone with my sweet wife, explaining my mystery condition and how "it hurts when my clothes touch it" and "it's hot to the touch" and "if I lay on my back, it feels like a thousand tiny needles."

She asked me to tell her again what I did that day, and I said, "Got off the plane, fell asleep in the direct sun for four hours, and then came to the hotel. Why? Do you think that has something to do with my radioactive back rash?"

She then spent the next few minutes on the phone with us explaining what to do next step by step. "Go to the store. You are looking for something called aloe vera."

My wife, Sami, healed my mystery back condition (which turned out to be a very run-of-the-mill thing that people experience every day). When I think about the way Sami has come into my life and what she has taught me about love and life (and sunburns), I can honestly say that in more ways than one, she has changed my life and saved my life. I always say that she was the mirror I needed to truly see myself and the world around me.

On May 13, 2017, I got to marry the most beautiful woman in the world. We threw the best party with 250 of our closest friends. I know it sounds cliché, but I can really say it was the best day of my life. Not only was it the best party I've ever been to with the most delicious tacos and ungodly amounts of tequila and all my favorite people, but it also felt extra sweet because of how hard we worked and how much we freaking fought to get there. When I met my wife, the odds of us making it to that day felt truly astronomical. Not because we didn't love each other or because of our own fear of commitment but because of how many people, lives, and structures it would disrupt for us to be able to be true to who we are. We grew up in the church and in a world that made it seem like man plus woman was the only true definition of marriage, which made it very hard to find our own path as two women who were so very in love. But standing there on that day, at the wedding of our dreams, made it all worth it. And not just for us.

Our good friend Brian (who you will hear more about in this book) was one of Sami's bridesmen. We all went to the same Christian college, and Brian actually came out a few years before us. If you ask anyone at our wedding what stood out to them or what they remember from the ceremony, they might talk about our vows or the music. But after they give you the obligatory "the girls looked beautiful," they'll probably mention how hard Brian cried. Brian was truly a mess in the best way possible, and because all of Sami's people were standing behind her and I was facing toward her, every now and then out of the corner of my eyes, I could see his shoulders shaking uncontrollably. It was the first same-sex wedding he had ever been to, and it meant so much to him. We have all joked many, many times about how hard he was crying, and I was definitely crying too. In fact, I saw so many people crying during our ceremony. While I want to imagine they were crying because the sheer magnitude of my physical beauty was just too much to handle, I think they were crying for reasons that are actually even more meaningful.

Just a few weeks ago, I finally asked Brian why he was crying so hard at our wedding. In the past, he had told us it was because it was his first gay wedding. This time we were having a drink, and he gave us an answer that brought me to tears (again). Not only did Brian, Sami, and I go to the same Christian college, but we also ended up at the same church after college. I was a pastor at the church, Sami worked in the creative department, and Brian attended. The church was only eight miles from the college we went to, so every Sunday was a bit of a reunion, with so many people from both areas of our lives coming together. But our college and church held something else in common, too: they were not places where it was okay to be gay. You couldn't work at either institution if you were gay, of course, but it went a little beyond that. Every person who called these places home was assumed (and required) to have a view of the world and of God that was not inclusive of people who were gay.

On May 13, when we stood in front of 250 of our closest friends, many in the audience had called these places home. So here's what brought Brian to tears: our wedding was at 5:00 p.m., meaning the sun was shining perfectly on us but really beating down on the crowd. Brian told us that as he looked out, he saw all those people from our church and from our small Christian college putting their hands on their foreheads, leaning in, and trying to block the sun from their eyes so they could see our wedding better. He really began to cry, he told us, when he realized that for years, many of those same people used those same hands to cover their eyes—not wanting to see or celebrate the lives of queer people—and now, they were using their hands to try to get a better view of two women getting married.

That is what evolution looks like, that is what change and growth look like, and that is what is possible when we run head-on into what scares us. Our choice to embrace freedom over fear will impact not only our lives but so many lives around us. Now, don't get me wrong—plenty of people from our college and church community didn't show up that day. Plenty of people we loved are still covering their eyes and do not want to see us. It took so many tears and gut-wrenching conversations and heart-filled therapy sessions to get to that day, but I would do all of it again in a heartbeat. If I have learned anything over these past few years, it is that just because something is hard and scary doesn't mean it's bad or wrong. Just because something is the right thing to do does not mean that it will be easy—but it will be worth it.

There's a familiar cycle of life that we all know and understand and witness: every fall, trees lose their leaves, only to grow new leaves again in the spring. (This analogy may be lost on you if, like me, you live in southern California, but trust me, seasons are a real thing.) Our lives are filled with similar cycles of loss and regrowth as well. Just think, every single minute we're alive, we empty our lungs only to fill them again. And yet, with all of this change and loss and growth built into the very nature of what it means to be human, we still tend to fear change and transition. We know that change and loss are often met by finding new life again, but that doesn't mean doing something new and stepping into change isn't going to be scary and often painful.

At some point, many of us stop being willing to risk the pain, so we stop changing and growing. We get scared of what people might think, conform to the path of least resistance, and look for perpetual sunshine instead of letting the natural seasons of life strip away what is dead and allow new life to grow. I'm here to tell you that in any season, at any point in our lives, finding new life—even though it may be painful—is worth it. A life lived in search of perpetual sunshine will cause us to miss out on some of the most beautiful experiences life has to offer (and as I now know, a life of perpetual sunshine will also burn your back). These days, when I wake up each morning and I see my sweet wife's face and we make breakfast and play with our dog, my whole life feels like spring—a spring that could not have emerged without a hard fall and a brutal winter. But I would live through those seasons a million more times if it means one million more springs. This book is about the incredible possibilities that await each of us. It's not just a coming-out story or the story of me and Sami. It's not just about leaving the church and the world I grew up in for the pursuit of love. It's a call to action for all of us, wherever you are and whoever you are, to become the people we are meant to be, even if that means hard seasons. I promise spring is coming, and spring is always, always worth it.

Some days when I wake up and see my wife's face, I am reminded of the fact that I almost didn't have any of this because of what other people might think about it. For so long, I allowed my fear of others' reactions to keep me from living as my true self. During the three years my wife and I spent in the closet, I considered *a lot* of very random people's thoughts and feelings. Here's just one example. When I was a teenager, my dad was the vice president of an organization called Promise Keepers—an evangelical organization for men that happened to be pretty conservative. One of my dad's coworkers also had a son around my age. Now, just for context, my dad stopped working for this organization over ten years ago, and I haven't seen my dad's old coworker's son probably since I was seventeen years old. This guy absolutely was not a definitive character in my life. I did not have his phone number, and we didn't follow each other on social media. Truly I feel like there could not have been more distance between two people. Yet, years later when I was deep in the closet, working through my own shame and fear, I probably spent an entire week thinking about this coworker's son, remembering how conservative he was in 2002, and wondering what he thought now and what he might say when word got back to him that I was gay and . . . what the hell what I talking about! When I look back now, from the perspective of my springtime joy, I truly mourn the fact that I could have been here sooner, but I was too busy obsessing over people like my dad's old coworker's son!

It's a ridiculous story, but I don't think I'm the only one who has obsessed over the reactions of others, especially the reactions of others who were not even a part of my life anymore. Maybe you haven't been in the closet and gone through a mental list of every conservative person you've ever known to try and guess what they might say, but you probably have compromised your vision of who you want to be in the world because of what other people might think about you. Maybe they were main characters in your life and maybe they were as peripheral as my dad's old coworker's son. Maybe they aren't even real people but just the voices you've heard from social media. Way too often, we are willing to compromise our truth and vision for people who aren't even invested in our lives. The harsh reality is that we are the ones who feel those consequences. I was the one who was in the closet for years. My dad's old coworker's son did not feel the repercussions of my choice. He is not paying my therapy bills; I am.

A friend of mine who has two kids was talking to me about how she never realized what a competitive sport motherhood would be. As a person with no kids, I guess I didn't realize either. But from the time she was pregnant, I have watched her as she moves through the world being constantly bombarded with very strong opinions from strangers. One day during her pregnancy, we went to the grocery store together, and no fewer than ten people randomly and aggressively offered her advice that she definitely did not ask for. I thought that phenomenon might end after she gave birth, but wildly, it only got more intense. By the time her kids were preparing to go to school, you would have thought she called a town hall meeting. All kinds of people had all kinds of thoughts—homeschool versus public school versus private versus charter versus dual immersion versus I don't even know what else. She told me how overwhelmed she felt because she didn't want to upset all those people.

But then she said, "At the end of the day, where I choose to put my kids in school and how I raise them is on me." She knew she would never be able to make everyone else happy. It was going to be her decision, and she was going to live with the consequences.

Too often we put our decisions on other people. Instead of trusting our own intuition, we allow others to define our lives for us. If I had stayed in the closet my whole life and told people, "I wanted to come out but my dad's old coworker's son made it impossible," you'd probably tell me that I had more agency over my life than I thought. Now it's time to look in the mirror. Though you may be unfairly bombarded with opinions, you have agency over your life too. You can choose to grow and evolve, or you can choose to stay small and manage the opinions of the people around you. One of the questions in my head that finally dragged me out of the closet was this: "Is my life a reflection of who I want to be, or is it a reaction to people I don't want to upset?"

Don't miss out, people. Don't compromise your vision for anyone. Your life cannot be about not upsetting people. That will be a lifelong human resources position with no pay, no benefits, and no time off. You are worth so much more than that. Yes, it will definitely be hard. Yes, some people may say and do very hurtful things, but winter is just a part of life and spring is always coming.

1

EVERY TIME I THOUGHT I HAD ARRIVED, I WAS WRONG

When I was in middle school and high school, I had to pretend to know *a lot* of things. My parents refused to let us have cable (lots of church plus frugal parents equals no cable), and the internet was not the ubiquitous entity it is today. I had to pretend to know about one million pop culture references to save myself from massive embarrassment. When I was in eighth grade, a very popular show on MTV called *TRL* (*Total Request Live*) aired the top ten most popular music videos of the day, and it was hosted by a man named Carson Daly. Carson Daly was a name I heard *so much* at school, but I had no idea who he was. I tried so hard to pick up on context clues to try and figure out who or what Carson Daly was. I didn't want to suffer the embarrassment of asking my friends, "Is Carson Daly a boy? A girl? A band? Do they go to our school?

Is Carson Daly someone famous or the name of our new principal?" This is what life was like before Google. Since I had no idea, naturally, I went to the source of all knowledge at the time. I asked my dad if he knew who Carson Daly was. He did not. But like a good dad, he pointed me in the direction of our basement, where we had a full set of encyclopedias. Yes, I have *that* dad. When my siblings and I were each around ten years old, he taught us how to look for answers in the two shelves full of huge burgundy and gold encyclopedias in our basement. These books essentially served as outdated Google for most of my adolescence. In a lot of cases, the encyclopedias were actually helpful. I used them for research for most school projects and to answer the occasional embarrassing human anatomy question (because sex ed was a sin, apparently). But I'm sure you won't be surprised to learn that early 2000s MTV personalities were not listed in our 1980s set of encyclopedias, so I just played along, pretending to know what a Carson Daly was until the next mystery came my way. And *a lot* of mysteries came my way without cable or the internet.

The other day I was having dinner with a group of friends and they were all joking and laughing as they shared their first AIM screen names. My wife's was *voteforpedro11* because she saw *Napoleon Dynamite* eleven times in the theater. My friend Katie had the handle *k8ieluvs2talk*, which perfectly prefigured her career as a public speaker. What was my first screen name, you ask? All I could offer the conversation was what my parents told me when I asked them if I could have AIM and chat with people online: "There's no one you need to know on the internet that you don't already know in real life."

Honestly, I am very grateful for that season of simplicity in my life, but I definitely missed out on a lot of cultural knowledge. If only I'd had access to something like Google so I could search things that I always wondered but weren't in the encyclopedia like, "Why does Nelly have a Band-Aid on his eye? Are thongs *supposed* to be worn so you can see them? Where can I buy a velour tracksuit?" The list of things that I was unsure about was long and vast.

The list of things I knew was a bit shorter, but I believed each of them with my whole heart. One of the things that I knew for sure at this point in my life was the difference between right and wrong. Right and wrong, I was taught, were clearly defined lines, and the map to a happy and fulfilling life was broken down in pretty simple steps. If everyone else would just get on board, the world would be a better place. Did anyone else grow up with this narrative? No? Was that just me?

Well, luckily for me, I peaked pretty early, and by the time I was a sophomore in college, I knew absolutely everything there was to know about everything. And funny enough, every other student in the sophomore class also knew all that there was to know in the universe. At the ripe age of nineteen, I knew what was right, I knew what was wrong, and I knew all of the decisions I needed to make that could lead me exactly where I wanted to go (heaven). This was the myth that the evangelical church preached—there was a right and a wrong way to live and if you lived the right way, nothing bad would ever happen to you and you could avoid any suffering.

Because I bought into this mindset, I rarely felt that I might be wrong. I had complete certitude about most of the beliefs in my life. It turned out that because most of my sophomore peers felt the same, I spent a lot of my time that year—and if I am honest, years before as well—vehemently defending my viewpoints against my peers who were equally sure about their opposite conclusions. These are positions that I now think are either completely unimportant or just flat-out wrong. I had strong beliefs about everything, from deep theological truths about who will and won't get to heaven (what a strange argument to have), to political views about the war in Iraq. (I don't know why the military just didn't reach out to me directly as I, a nineteen-year-old with literally no knowledge or experience, for sure had all of the answers.) Even with seemingly meaningless things, I defended my beliefs unconditionally. On one day I'll always remember, I got into an argument with a close friend about the war in Iraq and what we should do. Just to clarify, we were two nineteen-year-olds with exactly zero military experience between us and even less knowledge of war. We had the most minimal knowledge of politics, and we were going for it like it was a presidential debate. The argument got so heated that we didn't talk for like a week after. I was so sure, absolutely positive about my stance and my "plan" (it feels wrong to even assign the word *plan* to the uninformed gibberish I was defending at the time), but still, I felt sure. I felt like I had arrived and anyone who wasn't with me must have been wrong or misled. I couldn't make space in my world for anyone or anything that challenged the beliefs I held so close to my chest. Even my close friends became victims of the chopping block that was my unnecessarily rigid belief system.

If I felt that strongly about things I actually had no part in, then you already know I had some way stronger and far more rigid beliefs about God. My beliefs and certainty about God—the way God worked and the things God wanted me to do—were enormously comforting and helped everything make sense, at least for a while. I had an answer to every question. I knew the things I could do that would please God and make my life better, and I knew the things to avoid that displeased God and would make my life harder. I believed deep down to my core that God was keeping some kind of score. If I locked myself out of my apartment or got a bad grade on a test, I would attribute it to the time I cursed as I sang along to the part in "Hollaback Girl" by Gwen Stefani that says, "That's my shit, that's my shit." (Was anyone else obsessed with that song in 2005 or just me?) Or maybe it was that time I got drunk at a party and lied about it to my RA in the dorms. I believed that every move I made left me open for judgment, and a negative judgment meant punishment. If the price to pay for cursing or drinking was locking myself out of my apartment, then can you imagine the levels of hell that I thought might be waiting for me when I fell in love with a woman at the ripe age of twenty-seven—after over a decade of *knowing* that being gay was on the list on no-nos, and it was way above drinking.

Discovering and beginning to embrace my own sexuality led me to begin to question and pull on the threads that kept my whole worldview knit together, and that was so very terrifying. I had been absolutely sure of so many things my whole life, but then they all started to unravel. Looking back, I realize that some of my beliefs weren't holding up in my real life long before I realized I was gay. It is hard to hold onto a belief that God is keeping score and rewarding your good behavior because sometimes life just gets hard and you cannot avoid that with good behavior. When my grandma passed away and my friend from college got sick, I could not reconcile the fact that maybe these bad things were caused by my bad behavior. My grandma didn't die because I cheated on a test, made out with boys, and drank before I was twenty-one. My friend didn't get sick because they snuck alcohol onto our dry campus. These things happened as a part of life, but they didn't fit into the worldview I had built my whole life around and didn't want to question. I was at a Christian college, for Christ's sake! I was deep in this.

Eventually, I had to start pulling on these loose threads because I needed to know what was going to happen to me. This started to unravel the bigger picture, and I began to understand ways in which my beliefs and my worldview may have not been entirely functional. But—and I don't know if you can relate to this—even as those threads started to unravel and they didn't necessarily work anymore, they were still so comfortable that I didn't want to let them go. Even if they weren't working, at least I knew them and I knew how to have a life inside of them, so I tried to hold onto them.

I felt a sense of comfort believing that there was a way to live that would allow me to avoid being hurt and hurting others entirely. But then, of course, I hurt people and I got hurt, and that belief (along with others) started to deteriorate. For as long as I could, I ignored that tension because it felt like a problem, and for most of my life, I believed there was a way to give all of my problems to God, who would magically take away all of the stress, tension, and weight I carried. But as you may have guessed or probably experienced, that didn't necessarily work. Yes, I believe there is a God and that can be incredibly comforting in and of itself, but I just don't believe there is a magical equation we can access through good behavior, tithing, and church attendance that will allow us to avoid the suffering that is so fundamental to life. I found myself not actually believing the things I said I believed anymore, but I didn't know how to let them go because pretending to know it all still brought me so much comfort and security. I have been and am still on a long journey of trying to seek what is *true* rather than trying to be *right*.

I now believe that certainty is less of a comfort and more of a warning sign. The places in my life that start to feel rigid and nonmalleable have now become giant flashing lights telling me something might be wrong. If there is one thing this journey has taught me, it is that choosing freedom is about becoming, not arriving. **Every time I thought I had arrived, I was wrong.** Even now, when I find myself in incredibly open and inclusive spaces, the temptation to cling to certainty still seduces me. I am reading all of these progressive books and engaging with things like mysticism (things my nineteen-year-old self would have classified as "mumbo jumbo"). I love yoga, I diffuse essential oils, I get my tarot cards read, and my wife has a bunch of random rocks around our house that are supposed to somehow make us feel more calm, and I love it. These days the belief I cling to most closely is that people are good and deserving of love just as they are and that fighting for love is our most noble fight. But in reality, I still catch myself thinking and talking about certain people (*cough, cough,* conservative Christians, *cough*) in the same way I was upset at them for talking about me. I am throwing the same kind of stones, but now I am just throwing them from the other side (of course, they aren't stones; they are amethyst crystals that also reduce anxiety).

I think back to that moment in sophomore year, sitting across from my friend and trying so hard to convince them that I knew what to do about the war in Iraq. But I wonder what those arguments might look like today. Where in my life do I still cling tightly, and where have I allowed my grasp to open? I have learned to have open hands about many of the opinions I hold. I am not going to argue with you if you think Taylor Swift is the voice of our generation—good for you. If you need me, I will be watching "Lemonade" by Beyoncé for the thousandth time. But do you. I don't need to convince you that Beyoncé *actually* is the voice our generation has been waiting for. If you don't see that, okay. I can have an open mind.

It gets tougher when we stop talking about music and start talking about people. How do I not dehumanize someone because they dehumanize someone else? How do I sit across the table from someone who thinks my wife and I shouldn't be allowed to be married? How do I sit across the table and listen to someone who thinks it's okay to separate migrant children from their families? How do I not rage against the idea that men are somehow better equipped to do, well, everything apparently? I think these are things we need to do. These are corrupt systems that need to be confronted and dismantled, but how can we do that without becoming the very things that have hurt us? How? I don't know the answer. But I am trying more every day to learn.

I *know* how painful it is to sit at a Thanksgiving table or at a birthday dinner or backyard happy hour with people you have loved dearly and watch them as they wrestle to understand your very existence. I know how painful it is to be scrolling social media and be confronted with images of people who look like you being targeted and killed just for existing in the world. I know how scary it can be to move through the world as a woman when there are men who feel entitled to you. This world is harsh sometimes, and we don't always (or often) deserve the hardships we face. Our challenge is to respond to the harshness of the world without being harsh right back.

Growing up in the evangelical church, I obviously grew up hearing a lot about Jesus. Now please feel free to have your own thoughts and ideas or beliefs about who Jesus was and what that means for you. But there is one part of the story I was taught that has become more revolutionary to me in recent years. At the end of Jesus's life is a crucifixion, and I was always taught to feel bad for Jesus for how badly they beat him up. Yes, I saw *Passion of the Christ* and it looked bad. But I think this whole story had something much more powerful for me hidden in it. It's not just someone saying, "Feel bad for me," but it's someone saying, "Watch me take on all the violence without giving violence in return. Watch me take on oppressive systems without becoming an oppressor."

Though we don't live in a place that is still regularly crucifying people on crosses, most of us know what it is like to be tempted with the reality that we can hurt people in the same way we have been hurt. We have the option to return violence with violence. We can become so angry and upset about the injustice around us that we become unjust. It is a very fine line, and I think we have the opportunity to learn from Jesus and say, "Even though I have been hurt, I will not pass that same hurt on." That's the power of transformation.

I still feel certain about some things. I feel certain that all people deserve to be as they are. I believe in love. I am certain of my pursuit of freedom, and I am trying as hard as I can to confront oppressive systems without becoming oppressive and to heal from my own hurt without hurting others. We cannot always avoid pain, but we can always choose how we respond to that pain. Since we are going to be here, since we are going to have to confront hard things, **since we are going to have to**

move through pain, we might as well do it with open hands and see what we pick up along the way.

I know I haven't arrived yet, and I am okay with that. I just know what I want to move away from. I don't have all the answers, and I don't get to hurt people just because I am hurting. I am simply trying my best to be open to as much change as possible. And change sometimes means loss.

The truth is, none of us will ever "arrive," so that means we will always be growing and changing and evolving. That's not something to avoid. We don't need to dig our heels deeper into the sand every time we feel the ground shift. It's okay to shift with it. It's okay to change your mind. It's okay to be a different person than the one you were ten minutes ago. **The ground is shifting, and it's okay to let it move you.** I can tell you from experience that the feeling of freedom that comes when you commit to a life of evolving and change is far better than anxiously trying to protect your rigid and possibly failing beliefs. I've always been inspired by a quote from James Baldwin: "I imagine one of the reasons people cling to their hates so stubbornly is because they sense, once hate is gone, they will be forced to deal with pain."[1] I get it. It's hard to see the ground shift beneath the house and the world you've built on it—especially if you've treated people poorly because of it.

---

1. Baldwin, *Notes of a Native Son* (Boston: Beacon Press, 1955), 101.

It may feel easier to just double down, stand your ground, and speak your truth even if you don't believe it because letting that thing go would mean you dealing with the pain underneath. I say let it go; it's not serving you anymore, sis.

Many people in my life whom I love still hold onto beliefs that no longer serve them because they fear what might happen if they open their hands to new possibilities. I understand how scary it is to begin to unravel those threads. But it has been incredibly painful to watch because we simply aren't meant to live with closed fists.

It is hard to watch my friends crumble under the anxiety and shame they feel for failing to live up to the rigid boundaries they've set up for themselves. I have friends who have believed that sex outside of marriage is wrong since they read a Joshua Harris book as a teen and signed a pledge card. Now they find themselves in loving, healthy sexual relationships in their thirties that they are ashamed to talk about. Even though their narrow definition of acceptable sex does not work for their lives (and also, fun fact, isn't even in the Bible), they cannot let it go. I have watched friends come out to their parents, who desperately want to love and embrace them, but the parents' rigid beliefs won't let them. They choose to keep the comfort of those beliefs over the love they have for their child. I have felt the pain of what it is like to leave the security and the comfort of something you built your whole life around.

For some of you reading this, the choice between closed fists and open hands seems like a no-brainer, but it's not really—especially for those of us who know the comfort of having answers who are still healing from the trauma that comes from letting it all go. But damn, is it worth it. It is worth it to live with open hands for the moment God fills them with something you could never have seen coming.

I am living a life that I literally never could have imagined. I used to think that being a pastor at a big church and traveling around to speak was the absolute biggest dream for my life—my definition of success. But when I came out, I had to let it all go. I had to give up my dreams and my definitions of success. I had to move forward with open hands and no idea what would fill them. Sometimes my wife and I look at each other and just laugh because our lives are so ridiculously good and filled with things we never knew were possible. Sami travels all over the world photographing artists and events and people, and I get to speak on bigger stages than I'd ever dreamed of and be a pastor of a small and perfectly weird church. At the end of the day, I get to make dinner for my wife and sit and dream about starting a family. My life isn't easy or perfect and is definitely not void of hard things, but it is real and true and good and *mine,* and it is also filled with millions of little moments that bring me deep joy and gut-wrenching gratitude because I didn't know how good it could feel. But to get here, I had to let go.

It is worth it to feel the freedom of not having to live on the defensive. It is worth it because letting go opens up new questions, new conversations, and new depths of what it can mean to be human. I don't think we are meant to be sure, and maybe we should stop praising certitude and start questioning it. **The playbook of humanity isn't about arriving, only becoming, changing, and evolving.** So take the risk, open your hands, and get ready to discover something new.

2

THE CAST THAT
EXPANDED MY STORY

The single quickest way to break ourselves out of a false sense of certitude—to create a bigger story in our lives—is people, especially people whose experience is completely unlike our own. Loving people has the power to expand the story in all of our lives. My best friend in middle school, Sandra, had a cousin with special needs. His name was Chris, and Sandra loved him fiercely so I loved him fiercely (because when you're twelve and your best friend does something, you do it too). Loving Sandra, Chris, and their whole family gave me a perspective I would never have had otherwise. Chris was the first person I knew with special needs. Knowing him while going through what was potentially the most judgmental time of my life—middle school—gave me a new lens for the way I interacted with all of the students at our school. Watching Chris move through the world while also hearing the things some of my classmates were saying about him created so much tension inside of me and taught me, among many other things, the power of my words.

I'll always remember that Chris gave the best hugs, and it brought him so much joy to give them. This kid would hug anyone and everyone! Hugging in middle school was awkward, because we were all still figuring out our bodies. Hormones, growth spurts, voice changes, you name it—everything about who we were at that age made things like hugs taboo. But not Chris. If you saw him and you were still ten feet away, he would already have his arms out in his signature style. One day I saw Chris from a distance in the hallway, and as soon as our eyes met, he reached out his arms. On my way over to him, I could see kids behind him, mocking the way he reached out his arms for a hug. I will never forget how terrible it was to watch these kids mock his arms and his voice and take everything good and pure about the way he wanted a hug and make it so awful.

Middle school is also the time when you start pushing the boundaries with words—including the words you use and cool new words you don't even know the meaning of but use anyway. It's also the time when some incredibly hurtful language starts to get thrown around like confetti. I remember starting to make connections about language and people because of Chris. There were some words that I already knew were off limits—the F word, the B word—but then I started hearing the R word a lot, and it just didn't sit right. I had no language for it, but I remember realizing that word was connected to a person I loved, and that didn't feel okay. Hearing that word immediately brought back the image of those kids standing behind Chris and mocking him while he waited for a hug, and I hated it.

Chris's story expanded the story for me and created a space for me to be more thoughtful and more understanding. He also gave the best hugs in our school, and I am grateful for that too. Chris was different but not in a way that challenged the rigid boundaries of my belief system. As I got older, I realized that expanding my perspective and loving some people had the potential to conflict with what I believed about God in a way that loving Chris did not.

Growing up in the evangelical church in the '90s, we were taught that certain behaviors were definitely off limits, including (in order from bad to worse): smoking cigarettes, drinking alcohol, sex before marriage, and being gay. Our youth pastors had pretty decent answers for why smoking and drinking were bad for you: smoking hurts your lungs, and if you drink and drive, people will get hurt. Even their admonitions against sex before marriage made a sort of sense since all (heterosexual) sex carries a risk of pregnancy. But being gay was labeled the worst sin without much explanation. You just knew it was bad and apparently so bad that you didn't even need to explain why. Was the health of my lungs at risk? If I drove while gay, would someone get hurt? I knew that the chance of unexpected pregnancy went way down with partners of the same sex, so what was the problem? I had no answers. I was just supposed to know that it was wrong and that was it.

I went to an incredible public high school in my neighborhood in Colorado. I had amazing friends and got a great education. The principal of our school won Colorado Principal of the Year two years in a row. Her name was Dr. Jarvis, and she was the only openly gay principal in our entire state. She was kind and fair, cared about the students, and rocked the hell out of a different pantsuit every day. Because we had an openly gay principal, our school became the only school in the district with a gay student club—HHART, Homosexual and Heterosexual Alliance Reaching for Tolerance. (Yes, the name sounds awful now, but remember, we are talking about 2001 in Aurora, Colorado, and LGBTQ wasn't the standard terminology.) As a result of this club, LGBTQ students were far more visible in our high school than any other. I knew a few students who lived way out of our district but petitioned to go to our high school just to be a part of HHART.

Because of Dr. Jarvis and HHART, I had the privilege of having openly gay friends in high school—brave teenagers who had the courage to be out in suburban Colorado in the early 2000s. But unlike my experience with Sandra and Chris, I struggled to embrace and accept those friends because of what I had been taught. Ironically, following my instinct and loving people got more confusing the more God was involved. I loved all of my gay friends from school and loved being around them, but I knew that for some reason, my faith made it complicated for us to be friends. Because of this tension and being confused about it all, truly, when I was at school, I felt somewhat ashamed to be a Christian.

I remember a huge event when I was in school called See You at the Pole. For some reason, on a pre-determined day, all of the Christian students would show up early before school started and gather around the flagpole to pray. I honestly do not have enough space in this book to unpack the unholy alliance between Christianity and nationalism this event illustrates. But I remember I would show up and pray, and as soon as we were done, I would try to rush out of there so people wouldn't see me. Whether you grew up in the church or not, in 2001 everyone knew that Christian was synonymous with antigay, and I was ashamed of that. I was living in two worlds. Even though I was a bit ashamed of my faith, I also relished the security and identity my faith offered me, so much so that I often let my faith override my empathy.

Time for a shameful story. When I was in high school, the phrase, "That's so gay" was used for literally everything;

"I don't like these shoes. They're gay." "Ugh, you don't want to come over and play PlayStation later. You're gay." "Come on, hurry up. Stop being gay." I actually cringe as I write this now, but I used this word like it was money and I was Jeff Bezos. I had an unlimited supply. One day, one of my friends who happened to be gay and out as a fourteen-year-old (he was already so brave) decided to confront me on my language. He did it in the most thoughtful, compassionate, and honest way possible.

He simply said, "Hey, when you say, 'That's so gay' when you're talking about something you don't like or something bad, it hurts my feelings as a gay person because it feels like you're talking about me."

Seriously, he was the most mature fourteen-year-old in the history of the earth. Do you know what I said in response? Did I thank him for his honesty and bravery? Did I promise then and there to never use that word again? Did I ask him if I had offended him in any other ways? Nope.

I said, "I don't even mean it like that. Don't be so gay about it."

Yep, the absolute worst response in the history of responses. I fumbled a perfect pass. (But, I mean, several years later the joke was on me . . .) You know what breaks my heart still as I think about this thing that happened literally almost twenty years ago? My lack of compassion for him was so different than my compassion for Chris. But why? When I look back on that moment, I realize the narratives I had been taught about people like my friend had allowed me to take his feelings less seriously. Once I built a bond with Chris and began to value him, I don't think the R word ever came out of my mouth again. But when my gay friend compassionately challenged me about using the word *gay*, I was able to dismiss it.

This is why **the stories that we tell about people matter.** High school was such a confusing time because even though I was trying my best not to let anyone find out what I believed, my beliefs were still guiding my actions. I remember feeling truly sad some nights, wondering whether all the sweet friends I knew and loved from HHART were going to hell. My heart still sinks when I remember those feelings. I couldn't fully love the people right in front of me because of my love for God and the small story that the church handed to me about who is in and who is out. I had empathy and compassion for too narrow a group of people, and I lacked empathy for too many.

It took me being on the outs to eventually realize that those boundaries never actually existed. When I came out, many of the people who claimed to love me suddenly cast me outside their circle of empathy and love. Once I claimed my identity as *both* gay and Christian, I understood that there are actually no barriers to love, no barriers to God, and no people who deserve less of our empathy because of who they are. **Whenever we choose to let our love for people expand the story, we're on the right track.**

For a lot of us who grew up in the church, we may have been handed a story that did have loving people as the ultimate goal. In many cases, the story of God that the church handed us not only made it difficult to love others, but it also made it almost impossible for us to love ourselves. When we aren't allowed to look around and honor the complexity in the people we encounter, how are we ever supposed to look inside and honor the complexity that exists within ourselves? Even my own complexities were so confusing to me that it wasn't until I turned thirty that I truly started loving the part of me that loved a woman. I'm still figuring out the complexities of my identity and selfhood. But the work and the journey are the point of it all. I don't think it matters when you start or even how many times you have gotten it wrong. Allowing your own complexities to show themselves and be loved is so important. I often shrink when I remember my friend in high school who so bravely and kindly offered me a larger understanding and how I shut it down. I still sometimes think about how I used to believe that it was a sin to be gay or that men are naturally better leaders than women. I *believed* these things. I believe differently today, all because I allowed myself to be changed by the people I encountered—because I trusted my partners on this evolutionary journey. Even though I have missed the mark so many times, continuing on this path is still worth it.

Every week at our church, New Abbey, we make everyone hold hands and are reminded that when we make a connection with someone who is different from us, all of our individual stories come together to tell a bigger story of who God is. But it doesn't stop there. If we can learn to love the person whose hand we are holding—including all of his or her nuances and complexities—we can learn to love our own complicated stories, too. **The quickest way to put distance between you and your neighbor, you and your friend, and even you and your enemy, is to keep that same distance between you and yourself.**

If we want to be a part of this evolutionary process, if we want growth and change, if we want to be more empathetic, kind, and compassionate people, then it is absolutely necessary to surround ourselves with people who can push the boundaries of our limited individual perspective. It is the people around us who shape what we understand and see as normal, and loving someone who can expand that story for you is the absolute fastest way to grow.

I feel so privileged to be alive in this time and place in history where we have nearly unlimited resources at our fingertips to be able to encounter people whose life experiences are completely unlike our own. When I first came out,

I realized that my experience, knowledge, and understanding of the LGBTQ community did not really encompass the trans experience. A lot of people around me felt the same. This was a part of our community that I wanted to know more about. I wanted to know how to advocate for them and try to better understand them. You know what's great about being alive today? The internet. I opened my computer and Googled "top trans advocates to follow on Instagram." Wouldn't you know it, the first article that popped up said, "Ten Trans Advocates That You Need to Follow Right Now." I clicked on the article, scrolled down, and followed every single one.

Every person who is different from you in some way does not automatically have a responsibility to become our teachers. Let's not perpetrate that narrative. However, there are so many people right now who are ready and willing to use their platform and share their experience in the world so we can expand our stories. I am so grateful for things like social media and for all of the people who have been willing to take me on a journey so I can begin to understand an even bigger, more expansive, and more inclusive story about gender. Growth, change, and evolution are foundational parts of what it means to be human. I think we understand this early on. Babies crawl, and then they hold onto things and stand up. Then they try walking, and all along the goal is for them to keep moving forward. If you have ever been around a little baby who is learning how to walk, you've seen the adults around them damn near throw a parade at every new step they take. But at some point in our lives, we realize that instead of cheering us on, the people all around us are just screaming, "Don't change. Don't grow. Don't expand the story." Staying the same was never the goal. Humanity has always evolved, and there have always been people who have pushed the boundaries or crossed the barriers and stood in the gaps. If your goal is to expand the story, if you are looking for someone to stand and fill in a gap or push the boundaries of the way you understand the world, then just start looking. Start asking, start reading, and follow different people on social media. There is such a vast world out there, and we are privileged to live in a time with so much access. Don't waste it by only engaging with people who are just like you. That's not how we grow.

3 LESS DEFENDING, MORE BEING

When I was in sixth grade, for whatever reason, I decided that this was my year to tap dance. My poor parents. Not only was I literally awful at it, but those shoes were so loud and I would insist on practicing on any hard surface in our house. But I stuck with it for an entire season, and at the end of the season, we had a recital. If you have ever been in dance, you know that the end-of-the-year recital is a big deal. So many parents spent months sewing sequins on socks, wristbands, and decorative headwear to make sure it paired nicely with our sequined leotards. Everyone looked forward to this Broadway-like production.

In the weeks leading up to the recital, we all got lists of things we had to wear to appear uniform when we got up there and danced our hearts out to the tap version of "Rockin'

Robin." On the list of things we needed was nude tights. "Nude" is used to describe a color that makes white people look like they are not wearing tights at all. But nude tights wouldn't achieve the same effect on my skin. I will never forget getting those tights, putting them on, and looking in the mirror, only to find that my legs were now about four shades lighter than the rest of my body. It looked and felt ridiculous, as if I were walking around with glow sticks holding me up.

When I got to the rehearsal, wearing my new glow sticks, one of my friends from the dance team said, "Huh, I guess nude isn't nude for everyone."

Yes, Shelly, welcome to my world. Nude is not nude for everyone. I really do think that was the first time sweet Shelly had to expand her imagination to include the experiences of people of color. Everyone else in our neighborhood and on the dance teams and in our schools was white. Putting those tights on felt like a physical representation of the tension that I felt every day. That was my first and my last year in dance. It wasn't only because of the tights—the fog machine at our recital gave me an asthma attack on stage, so there was not a lot of hope for my dance career for many, many reasons.

I grew up as a black woman in a predominately white neighborhood and school in suburban Colorado (a place not known for its diversity). Being black and being a woman are identities that have always sat at the forefront of who I am.

Those identities are visible. They are with me in every room I walk in, and they have shaped so many of my experiences. And at some point, I had to both address and fight the temptation to defend those identities in every room I walked in. I still find myself doing that often, even today, but I realized that sometimes just existing as a woman of color in a room is powerful. I don't need to perform or teach or explain; I can just be. To be honest, I think that is the most powerful experience for all of us. **Being in a room just as we are is a revolutionary act.**

When I was ten years old, before my dance career ever got off the ground, I was obsessed with the *Mighty Ducks* trilogy, which are three of the greatest movies ever made, and you can fight me on that. Each movie has roughly the same plot: a bunch of misfit kids get together, play hockey, and find unlikely success. I wasn't the only kid obsessed with these movies, and all of a sudden there seemed to be a relatively new craze for roller hockey. I know the *Mighty Ducks* start out as an ice hockey team but we had limited access to ice hockey rinks, so we settled for roller blades and traffic cones as goals. Maybe it was just the kids in my neighborhood, but either way, we were obsessed. Every day after school, I would come home, throw my stuff in the house, grab my roller blades, hockey stick, and knee pads, and head into the street to play hockey with the rest of the neighborhood kids until the street lights came on.

One day, I followed the usual routine, but something was different. So you can understand this change, let me to tell you about the kids on our block. There were about nine kids who lived on our street: seven boys and two girls. My best friend, Crystal, and I were the lone girls in this wild pack of neighborhood kids. On this very important day when I went outside, I found all of the boys wearing matching jerseys with their names on them. Can you imagine my jealousy? Not only did their jerseys have names on them, which was the pinnacle of success for any ten-year-old, but they were hockey jerseys! It had only been my lifelong dream (that year) to be a professional hockey player. (Sadly, I eventually found out there are no professional hockey leagues for children.)

I asked the boys where they got their jerseys. They told me that they were all signed up for a roller hockey league and were going to play games against other teams (also an important childhood success measurement). Then the bomb dropped. They told me that I could play with them after school on our street, but I couldn't be on the team because I was a girl. Now, I don't want to brag, but I was damn good at roller hockey. I was easily better than half those boys, so it just didn't make any sense that I couldn't be on their team. So I did the only thing that I knew how to do: I ran home and told my mom.

My mom is a truly wonderful human being and an outstanding mother. She does not mess around when it comes to her babies. When I told her that the boys wouldn't let me join their team, she calmly said, "Don't worry." She picked up the phone and made some calls. (Honestly, I would *not* have wanted to be the hockey coach on the other end of that call with my mom.) The next thing I knew, I had a jersey, and I was on the team! To be honest, Crystal was already over the hockey craze and didn't especially want to be on the team, but we were proving a point as young feminists, and I made her do it with me.

I remember showing up to practice and then to the games. Everywhere I looked, Crystal and I were the only girls—not just on our team, but in the entire league. I love what that experience taught me. Not only did my mom consistently model true advocacy in my life, but it also taught me how strong I was. I loved scoring goals on all of those boys. Every time I scored felt like some sort of payback for their false assumptions that girls can't play hockey. This whole experience was so meaningful for me in so many ways, from the way my mom advocated for me to playing my roller hockey heart out and feeling the joy of doing it to prove a bigger point than just winning. It was all so special to me that I still have my jersey to this day.

But there is something else that experience taught me. That roller hockey team was the first time I can remember exactly what it felt like to have to defend my existence. I was a girl on this roller hockey team and that meant something. I was always aware of that fact and it shaped the way I played and how hard I tried always needing to prove that as a girl, **I deserved to be there.**

And I've had to keep defending my existence. After being the only girl on the roller hockey team, I was the only black girl on the dance team and then the only black girl on the field hockey team in high school. (There is an unexplainable hockey theme in my life.) I was the only black student in a lot of my advanced placement high school classes. Growing up in suburban Colorado, I was the only person of color almost everywhere I went. Having to defend my existence in a space began to feel like second nature. I was very aware when I was the only one in a space, whether that was the only girl, the only person of color, and as I got older, the only gay person.

It took me many years and lots of therapy before I could identify that feeling directly. I remember sitting in my therapist's office telling her all of the reasons why I could not come out until I finally blurted out, "I'm already a black woman." It was as if I had finally acknowledged the weight I had carried for twenty-eight years of defending my existence, and it felt far too heavy to add anything else on. I had always felt the need to represent more than just myself. I had to represent all the girls who wanted to play roller hockey and all the black girls who wanted to dance and just wanted some damn tights in their color. I felt the expectations of generations of women and people of color who had come before me and fought for me to have the life I do now. Now sitting there, with this deeper understanding of my own sexuality and this woman I loved, I finally had to come to grips with the reality that it might be time for me to do less defending and more being.

If I am being completely honest, no place made me defend my existence more than the church. No phone call from my mom could prove to generations and generations of men that women deserved to speak on stage just as much as men did. A different-colored pair of tights wasn't going to repair the damage that misuse of the Bible had done to generations and generations of people of color. As a young woman who grew up in the church only to defy odds and become a pastor, defending my existence in every room was just the name of the game.

I will never forget sitting in a meeting where we were planning for a Sunday service that would feature a woman speaker. The male senior pastor reminded her that she needed to really prepare because she was going to get judged more harshly. "Make sure they have nothing they can say. Make sure you are prepared. Don't miss a step." This was how things worked. If you wanted to be a woman in this space, you had to be damn near perfect. It was exhausting. But then I realized something: I don't have anything to prove to these men! If you don't want to listen to me, don't listen. If you don't want to take me seriously, then don't. And if you think I need to prove myself to you, think again.

When I finally came up with the courage to come out, it kind of felt like I was graduating from school. You know how when you're in school, the principal dictates everything you do. You need their permission to start a club or join a team or to assess your intelligence. You even need to ask someone's permission to go to the bathroom. It's wild. But graduation means there is no more principal. You do not answer to them anymore, and you do not need their permission to live your life the way you want to. We all have had far too many "principals" in our lives telling us what we can and cannot do. Whether we realize it or not, I think a lot of us have graduated, but we are still seeking their approval and their permission.

When I was in college, the president of our university was a man named John Wallace. For six years (four years of undergrad and two years of grad school), that name meant so much to me. It was his seal of approval I sought, and at the end of it all, a handshake from him as I walked across the stage was the only thing that legitimized all of my work at that institution. That name carried so much weight in my life. Then one day, after I got that handshake, I got a job somewhere else and realized that the name John Wallace meant nothing to my coworkers. Ninety percent of the people in my life now had no idea who he even was. A name that had meant so much to me for so long now carried no weight in my life. It was oddly freeing. For six years I was working for his recognition, but now I had to find my own path.

Less defending and more being means not stopping to ask anyone who you can be. You just are. It looks like realizing that the powers that be were never in charge of you. It looks like going to the bathroom whenever (and wherever) you want to go and not giving a damn.

Since coming out and becoming a pastor at an affirming and loving church, I regularly encounter something that breaks my heart. I get message after message and go on coffee date after coffee date with people who are queer or progressive or in some way have broken out of the box that was constructed for them. So many of these people have asked me the same question: "How do I get the people in my life to love and accept me now that I have changed?" Let me tell you something—it is absolutely gut-wrenching to sit across from people who are spending so much energy defending their very existence. As much as I wish I could give them a magical formula or a script they can use, what I actually think is that maybe defending themselves shouldn't be the goal. Maybe life would start to feel different with a little less defending and more being. Even as I write that, I know they are super easy words to say but extremely difficult words to live. **But I have found there is so much life and freedom in just being.**

I can assure you all that you have graduated. There is no one you need to prove yourself to, and living for the approval of others will only result in more fear. It will never be enough. You want to push boundaries and make change and challenge systems? Good! But do it for you. Living to change people's minds is a nasty business, and I don't wish that on anyone. Whether it's the church or your family, your coworkers, or random people from high school—whoever it is you are trying to prove yourself to, what would it look like if you stopped? Choosing to be who *you* want to be rather than trying to be who *they* want you to be is the most important bridge we can build and cross in our lives. Let's start building. The world needs you to be the unique person you are. Stop defending your existence and show us how to be here.

I have started to think that there are two types of people in the world: people who work out with their shirts on and people who work out with their shirts off. Men, you have your own issues but I'm not talking about you right now, okay? I'm talking about women who work out in sports bras in the SoulCycle class or yoga class or whatever trendy and expensive (but worth it) way you like to sweat. You might assume that the major determining factor between these two groups of people is the weather; it is not. We would all be lying to ourselves if we said that taking your shirt off or leaving it on is a result of how hot you are. Listen, have you ever been to SoulCycle? It's like being in Mississippi in August; everyone is hot.

For most of my life (like, my entire life until a few months ago) I was the kind of person who never took her shirt off while working out. I don't have the body that most "take your shirt off" women have, so I would just pour ungodly amounts of sweat into my clothes and call it a day. I never even really thought about it. One day my wife and I were in hot yoga—a class that, just to clarify, is intentionally at deathly levels of heat. We got in and set up our mats. I looked to the left as my wife took her shirt off to reveal her perfectly fitting sports bra and athletic form. Then I looked to my right, and there was this wonderfully magical black woman who was full bodied and beautiful. She took her shirt off too. I looked around the room and saw the common theme I always see: skinny girls, no shirt; bigger girls, shirts. But not this woman. She had a look in her eyes that said, "I don't give a fuck about your body standards. This room is hot as hell, and I'm not gonna suffocate today." Standing in the presence of this woman gave me all kinds of inspiration, and I threw my shirt off too. It felt so free!

Maybe this sounds ridiculous to you, but I guarantee someone is reading this who has never felt like they are "allowed" to work out in their sports bra. Well, fuck that! And listen, sometimes the power of just being requires a little help. This woman offered me something I couldn't have gotten on my own, and I can't thank her enough for it. (No, I didn't actually thank her. I couldn't find a non-creepy way to say, "Seeing you made me take my shirt off.") In the business of less defending and more being, if you are struggling, get yourself around some strong women who will show you what it feels like. If you have found the freedom to just be in a space, then share it. And for God's sake, if it is ninety degrees or hotter, take your damn shirt off and be free. **Let your body just be, let your success be for you, let your ambition be your driver—not your revenge.** Fight the system, topple the patriarchy, do it all—but remember that you don't have anything to prove to anyone else.

4 CHOOSING FREEDOM MEANS CHOOSING CHANGE

Coming out to my parents was absolutely terrifying. There is no better way to describe it. I knew without a doubt in my mind that my parents loved me. They truly are the best parents. We had a great relationship. I adore them, and they adore me. This was by far the biggest secret I had ever kept from them, but I just could not find the courage to speak those words to them. I am not sure exactly what I was afraid of except definite and imminent change. Everything was going to change. I remember one night, staying up late and talking to Sami, dreaming and sharing our fears, and realizing that almost all of my biggest fears came down to change. I didn't want the way my parents looked at me to change. I didn't want the way people looked at them to change. I didn't want any of it to change. But the truth was, it already had.

One night when Sami and I were up late talking again, I broke down into tears. All I could say was, "I have to tell my parents." I just had to. I wanted them to know me. I wanted to know what they thought and what they might say. I wanted to share this with them so badly. I just had to tell them. I went over to their house for breakfast the next morning, and my mind was reeling. I have never questioned my parents' love, but this was going to certainly ask for them to make some pretty significant evolutionary jumps. I didn't just randomly wander into the evangelical church scene as a child. I was there because my parents were there, and they were there because they believed in it. They still did . . . I still did at this point. But what were they going to do when I told them that who I was didn't fit in that world anymore?

I sat down for breakfast, looked at them both, and just started sobbing. I could barely mutter out the words, "I'm in love with Sami." In their sweet faces I saw a touch of surprise but so much love. My mom was already crying. She had started crying as soon as I did, even though she had no idea why.

My dad looked at me with his very fatherly look, and the first words out of his mouth were, "We have always told you there is nothing you can do to make us love you more and nothing you can do to make us love you less, and we meant it. We love you."

I let out the biggest sigh of relief, and we all cried, my dad included. In those first minutes, I could see my parents' minds were reeling with all of the impending change that was coming their way. My mom got up and hugged me. Then through her tears she mustered out, "Just promise me you'll adopt or something." Because no matter what is going on, Mexican moms only have one thing on their mind at all times: grandkids. At that moment, we all started to laugh, and I assured my mom she would still get grandkids.

We sat around the table for the next hour. As the dust began to settle, new questions started to come up: "What are you going to do about your job?" I didn't have an answer. All I knew was that I couldn't keep my job and be who I was. As I look back, I realize that this question about my job was about way more than where I worked. "What are you going to do about your job?" was code for, "What are you going to do about the entire community that you can no longer stay in?" My job was church, and my job was community. My job was entirely wrapped up in a system and way of doing things that did not make space for this kind of change. I think my parents knew that all of the changes I was about to undergo would have to involve them too.

I will always have nothing but respect for my parents and the ways they have showed up, faced change, evolved, and loved us with a ferocity I didn't even know was possible. If you see my mom these days, she is most likely wearing a rainbow something as a part of her outfit. She may have a rainbow pin on her jacket or a rainbow on her phone or earring or bracelet or shirt. She is all in. She has been a mom figure to so many LGBTQ folks whose parents did not choose the road of evolution. If you see my dad on a Friday, he is probably wearing the same shirt he wears every Friday. It says, "Be Free." An organization that started giving out these shirts as a way of signaling that you are a safe person to come out to. My dad calls it "Be Free Friday."

My parents' love for me has shaped who I am. I could not be more proud of the way they have faced this change head-on. But it has been by no means easy for them. Their evangelical friends and church community who did not embrace the change made this process extremely difficult for them. They have experienced so much loss. They have lost friends they thought they would have forever, and they lost a church community that they loved. They have had difficult conversation after difficult conversation, and honestly, I think that is why most of us fear change. **It's not always about the change itself, who we will become, or what it might teach us. I think most of us are afraid of the loss that will come along the way.**

While it didn't scare me as much as coming out to my own family, I was nervous about us telling Sami's family too—especially her grandparents. Sami has four living grandparents, while all of my biological grandparents have passed away. I think I was nervous about her grandparents because they'd lived longer in a world that fully rejected LGBTQ people. They were the ones whose worldview would be changed the most by our lives—the ones who we were asking to evolve the most.

One of my wife's grandmothers is named Frances, but nearly everyone calls her Fran. So, of course, my wife calls her Franma. Sami and Franma have one of those unique bonds. They are kindred spirits, born decades apart but made for each other. Franma is Sami's person, and I love watching their relationship. Franma is the epitome of the twenty-first-century grandma. She is always the first to comment on an Instagram story, Facebook post, or tweet from any of her grandkids, and every time we see her, she references some important pop culture event we haven't even heard about yet. She has seen the world change in so many ways and still has so much love in her heart that it can't be contained. Franma made the transition to loving us so seamlessly that she makes me feel as if she has always known we were going to be a part of her life. She was at every bridal shower and every celebration leading up to our marriage. She took tequila shots and danced her heart out at our wedding. She is our biggest fan on social media and in real life, and I love her. In addition to her fierce love for us, and literally every single member of her family, Franma is also in love with butterflies, which is why my wife has a butterfly tattoo on her arm.

It's a cliché, but I am going to say it anyway: butterflies have so much to teach us about change. When I think about my journey, my journey with Sami, my parents' journey, and even Franma's journey, I think about the butterfly on my wife's arm. Butterflies have all been on a journey, having been transformed from caterpillars to beautiful winged insects, freely flying from flower to flower. It's easy to look at butterflies and see how beautiful they have become, but that change was not easy. Change rarely is. The journey I have been on to find the freedom I have now was not all butterflies and rainbows and Franmas. I lived through some serious darkness and a period of hiding when I didn't know what was going to come out on the other side. That—permit me one more butterfly metaphor—is just like a caterpillar in their cocoon. They don't know what will happen when they emerge from that dark place; they only know that they had to leave their caterpillar life behind.

I wonder if they are scared that when they come out on the other side, there will be friends and family who were more comfortable with them as a caterpillar. I think about this all the time. I think about my own change, my parents, and Franma. I think about all of the pain and all that people have lost to evolve with us, and I imagine them pulling one another aside and whispering, "I just liked things the way they were before _____" (you fill in the blank). The reality is that sometimes change can be brutal, and the process of evolving can be painful. **But longing for the way things used to be will only keep us in the darkness longer.**

I know what it's like to stay in the cocoon too long. Sami and I always refer to the years of 2013 to 2016 as the fog. These are the years when we knew change had come. We knew we were in love and we wanted to be together, but getting there felt impossible. Instead, for a while we just tried to keep our "normal" lives going while everything was in fact changing. Actually, everything had already changed.

A friend of mine tells a story about the first Thanksgiving he spent with his family after he had grown out of the theology, beliefs, and worldview he was raised with and after his political beliefs had shifted beyond what was acceptable for his family. I remember him telling me, "I am just not going to say anything, and they will never know what I think."

You can imagine how well that worked out for him. I think we've all been there. We've all been in a place where we have changed, grown, learned something new, and embraced it. Then we find ourselves in situations with people who don't want us to change or aren't okay with change, so we sit and pretend like nothing is different. It's one of the most uncomfortable feelings. The dissonance in those moments is almost palpable.

I remember sitting in my office at my church job. I was in love with Sami and felt like it was the best thing that ever happened to me, but I couldn't share it with anyone around me. One day, I had to sit in a meeting where I listened to the leadership of the church explain how as pastors, we were not allowed to officiate gay weddings. We sat in a conference room and wrote a statement that we could use whenever we were asked to perform a gay wedding. I can still recall the nauseous feeling as my body tried to hold onto all that dissonance. My good friends and colleagues, people I loved, people I thought loved me, were saying things like, "It's just wrong, and we cannot be a part of it."

They were talking about me, and they had no idea. Sometimes I just want to go back in time, shake myself, and say, *"Get out of this cocoon!"* Just do it. Embrace this change. You are not a caterpillar anymore, and pretending like you are is only going to hurt you. Yes, the change is scary. Yes, I lost relationships with every single person in that room when I came out. But the truth is, they had already been lost. I was just holding on to something that felt real but was not. Even though everything changed and relationships were lost, I wake up every single day now with a freedom I didn't even know was possible. I would do it all over again and risk it all because what I have now is so very worth it. It blows my mind to think about the fact that I almost gave up everything I have now for people in a room whose names I can barely remember. I almost let the approval and disapproval of peripheral characters in my life keep me in a cocoon that was only hurting me—not them. I don't know what kind of change you are experiencing or what kind of cocoon you may be in, but I can promise you this: **You will find more life than you imagined on the other side. That doesn't make the change easy; it just makes it true.**

We fear change because of what we might lose or because of what relationships might shift, but the fact of the matter is, if your inner perspective or identity has already changed, then the train has already left the station and things are already different. You now have the choice to embrace that change or fight it. I'll be honest with you—both options are hard. But one leaves you more whole. Choose that one.

5 MOVE INTO YOUR FEAR

I am not claiming to be an expert on fear, but I have passed out on a ride (that shall not be named) at Disneyland that my friends assured me "was not that scary." In the photo they take on the ride, everyone is screaming with their hands up, and I look like I am asleep on some sort of antigravity machine. My arms and head are just floating weightlessly (because I am unconscious). My body hates heights. It's a fairly irrational fear, but I have quite a few of those. For example, as long as I can remember I have been inexplicably (but also, understandably) afraid of clowns. When I was younger and would turn off the lights in my room before bed, I would look over at the closet, and somehow the shape of my clothes seemed legitimately suspicious. My first thought was always, *There's a clown in my closet. How? Why? How long has the clown been hiding in there?* Of course, if I had stopped to think about those things long enough, I would have realized that no, my clothes did not turn into a scary clown when I turned off the lights, and yes, I was perfectly safe on this ride at Disneyland that also had a seven-year-old on it. This is what we call irrational fear. On the other hand, we have some rational fears. I'm afraid that if I ask this person out on a date, they might say no—rational. I'm afraid that if I run for student body president, I might lose—rational. I'm afraid that if I'm vulnerable with others, they might reject me—rational.

I lived so much of my life with a destabilizing fear of vulnerability. When it came to living openly and sharing myself with the people around me, I just felt paralyzed. I was in college the first time I went to therapy. (I went because it was free. If you are reading this and you are in college, please take advantage of free therapy. You will not regret it.) I remember telling my therapist that I was afraid that if people knew everything about me, they wouldn't like me anymore. I wasn't yet aware of my own sexuality, and to be honest, I didn't even know what I was so afraid people might find out. I just knew that I liked being liked, and I didn't want to jeopardize that.

I started to work through these fears and eventually learned that, while vulnerability is most certainly a risk, it is also totally worth it. (Thanks, Brené Brown.) And so I began to try to live my life more openly. As I became more open—to both others and myself—who I really was began to emerge. And you know what's scarier than thinking a clown is in your closet? Finding yourself in the closet.

Let's talk about fear a little bit. I have heard people say that fear is a liar. I get that some of our fears aren't based in reality but only the false narratives we've been led to believe. But we also have fears that *are* real. In either case, I don't know if fear is as much a liar as it is a captor. Some fears are real, but we have the choice about whether to let those fears hold us captive. Many times in my life, the things I was afraid of have actually happened. And you know what? I survived anyway. Those times have taught me so much about what fear really is.

I don't believe that fear is ever something you can escape. I don't think there is a point of arrival where you become a person without fear, and I don't think there is nothing to be afraid of in life. I simply think **we can choose to let fear control us or we can move through our fear.**

One of my deepest fears, for as long as I could remember, was that there would be something about me that people wouldn't like. Maybe, more accurately, I was worried I would be a poor reflection of the people around me, mostly my family. I always wanted to make sure that people knew how great my parents were or how kind my siblings are. I always wanted to be a good reflection of the work my parents put in to raise me. I never wanted to give people a reason to not like me or to think less of me, so being gay was truly a shitstorm of all my fears breeding with one another.

I remember trying to tell myself that maybe the things I was afraid of weren't real or weren't going to really happen. Maybe all of the conservative Christian people I knew would magically change what they thought about gay people because of me. Maybe I was just funny and charismatic enough to avoid any and all pushback. Maybe there was some way to come out while being a female pastor at a megachurch and still somehow emerge magically unscathed. It sounded ridiculous then, and it sounds ridiculous now. Change costs us, fear is real, but even when everything you fear happens, the person you'll become on the other side of those fears is a fuller version of yourself.

On top of all of my fears of wanting to be liked or wanting my family to be liked, I had a deep-seated fear of not being loved by God. I believed that the love of God was unconditional, the only constant, and being loved by God felt like the only thing people around me couldn't control. And yet, that love also felt deeply tied to certain people's approval of me. It felt like somehow pastors and church elders were handing out tickets for God's love, but you had to meet all the requirements first, like, "Must be this tall to ride," "Keep your hands and arms inside the car at all times," and "Do not be gay." It felt like even if you believed in your heart that God loved you, that didn't matter unless some kind of spiritual leader corroborated your story. If I was the only person who thought God loved me, was that even real? How would I know it was real? My confidence in God's love for me, for better or for worse, had mainly come from other people telling me it was true. Now I was on my own to figure it out. Instead of hearing endless affirmation of God's love for me, I was afraid I was about to hear an onslaught of voices saying the opposite. I wasn't even sure how to start to prepare myself to face the fear that maybe God did not really love me.

On one of my last days at my megachurch job, it was one of the last times I was around all of my friends and coworkers before I came out. It happened to be a staff worship day. The band from our church played worship music, and we were free to listen, pray, and take some time to recharge ourselves spiritually. I typically would have loved a day like this—finding a spot in the back, enjoying the incredibly talented musicians, and singing along to the music. (It would have been so loud that no one would ever know how terrible I sounded—my ideal musical environment.)

On this day, I felt so terrified that I barely even made it into the room. I can still remember how all the lights were dim, the room was dark, multicolored lights shone brightly, and there was even a touch of fog for added effect. There on the stage were all of these people I had come to love singing songs about how much God loves us, and I could barely stand. I was so overcome by the fear of what was coming next. Were these songs still true for me? I stood in the back and began to cry. I cried and cried until my mouth uttered the words, "Am I okay?"

I asked honestly and desperately, "Am I okay, God?" It was such a transformative moment for me because as soon as I let myself ask the question, I felt more peace than I had felt in a long time. I felt okay. I had been so afraid of that questions for so long that the simple act of allowing myself to ask it provided incredible relief. All I had to do was acknowledge my fear and allow myself to ask the hard question out loud, and I felt so much better.

I remember saying to myself, "Hold onto this. You're going to need it." I knew that I would need that moment for what came next. I would need that moment for the weeks following when the people in that room did try to take away my coupon for unconditional love. I would need that moment for the time when I was driving and turned on some worship music— because that is what usually calmed my heart—and then out of nowhere the worship artist said something like, "Break the chains of homosexuality." I would need that moment when I sat with people I loved who I thought would walk with me and they told me this was not what God wanted for my life. I would need that moment for every single time someone implied I was too biased to know whether God still loved me. I needed that moment for every time every one of my fears came true.

I needed that moment, and that moment did not let me down. **I needed to ask the question, I needed to find the answer, and I needed to become the person I became through all of it.**

After I came out publicly and let all of the internet know, I started getting a ton of messages. A few of the most comforting messages I received were from my dad's friend who had recently gone through a divorce and the daughter of the pastor of my childhood church. She told me about her experience with getting pregnant before she got married. They both sent me messages that said, "We get it. We know what it's like to all of a sudden be on the outside of something that you held so close."

My dad's friend told me about how many people he thought would remain loyal to him but didn't. Sarah (my childhood pastor's daughter) said the same thing. She talked about how many friends walked away and how hard it was. But she also talked about how good her life has been. They both talked about arriving at a place with less fragility. Even though it was vulnerable and hard, they no longer felt fragile. Their identity no longer felt dependent on the opinions and expectations of others. This is the kind of knowing that can't be taken away by any pastor, leader, friend, teacher, or anyone else.

Growing up in the church, being a pastor, and coming out is my particular story of facing my particular fears. I was afraid that I would lose friends, be thought less of, and be cast out. Your fears might be different, but they're just as real. We all have them. We are always growing, changing, and evolving. For some of us—well, for most of us—that evolution will take us out of our neat, tight box. It is terrifying to think about all of the things that leaving that box, or being pushed outside of that box, might mean. Let me offer you this advice: **if you realize that it's a box, you have already outgrown it.**

I know fear is scary. That is literally the definition of fear. But **one of the gifts of fear is that it offers us opportunities that we might not have otherwise had.** If I had not been pushed to my brink of fear in that dark worship space, I would still be allowing others to define for me whether I was loved by God. If I had stayed in the box that was tightly wrapped around me, I wouldn't have the incredible family that I have today.

Listen, fear is so real. I get it. Fear is not always irrational (some fears are very rational!), and it is not always a liar (some of your fears will come true). It can be oppressive, but it can also be a gift. What if you asked yourself the questions you were most afraid to ask? What kind of answers would you get? What kind of freedom would you find? What is on the outside of the box that you are afraid to leave? What would it mean to know you are loved because *you* know it, not because someone told you to know it? Go into the fear, ask the question, kiss the girl, leave the job, tell the truth. It will not be easy, but my God is it worth it.

6 FREEDOM IS RISKY

Even though I'm writing a book about overcoming fear, I think it might be worth noting that one of the reasons I have thought so much about it and worked so hard on it is because it is not something that comes naturally to me. I love comfort, I love the absence of tension, and I am way more afraid of a lot more things than my wife. If I could have overcome my fears a bit sooner and chosen freedom quicker, then we would have probably saved ourselves about a year or so of living in the closet. Sami was always ready to move faster than I was. She was always able to see further ahead than I was. **Choosing freedom is hard, but it helps when you can learn from someone else choosing it ahead of you.**

When Sami and I were both working at the same church, we knew we had to get out if we wanted to be together, but we didn't know how or when. We seemed to be stuck in an endless cycle. I remember sitting in therapy one week and telling my therapist that I felt like I didn't know how to choose Sami and not resent her for having to lose my job and our community. I didn't think I could choose my job and community without resenting all of them because they were the reason I had to lose Sami. I knew which one I really wanted, but I was so freaking scared. I was caught in a loop that had no end. Choosing freedom and choosing fear both felt impossible.

In the midst of the fog, a position opened up at the church that seemed like it was custom built and designed for our friend Brian. Brian is our friend I mentioned earlier who cried uncontrollably as Sami's bridesman in our wedding. Brian and Sami met in college when they were both on a twelve-day wilderness backpacking trip. (Apparently there are some people in the world who would categorize this as "fun.") While they were on this trip with a group of other people, the two of them just really connected, and a beautiful, long, and deeply meaningful friendship began.

About six months after the backpacking trip, in Brian's senior year of college, he decided to come out very publicly. Brian attended the same conservative Christian university that both Sami and I went to, and Brian had practically become the mayor of campus. He was involved in everything, he knew everyone, and I'm pretty sure there wasn't a girl on campus who did not have a Brian crush. Honestly, I think at one point I even had a crush on him.

The thing about Brian, besides his astonishing good looks, great hair, and great singing voice, is that he may just be one of the most positive, loving, and smiley people you could ever meet. His love for people is contagious. So, when Brian came out his senior year at our conservative evangelical college, he was met with a huge variety of responses. He was met with so much love and also so much difficulty. This is his story to tell, so I won't go into details. It is enough to know that coming out of college and that experience, Brian decided that he wanted to help people understand what it looked like for someone to be gay and love God. He started a podcast and a YouTube channel and was one of the first people I knew who was actively trying to bridge this divide. Brian was beyond gracious in his approach, and at times he was even willing to be in nonaffirming spaces to help them through difficult conversations.

This is a ridiculous thing to ask of a person: "Can you put your entire personal and romantic life on hold while I try to unpack some misplaced theological furniture?" No thank you. But at this point, Brian was willing to sit in the middle. So when this job opened at our church, we knew Brian was the one who had to fill this spot. Not only was this job made for him, but we (rather unfairly in hindsight) also wanted to use him to test the waters of how people at our church were going to address this issue when it had a real person attached to it.

Sami told her supervisor about Brian and his experience and all the ways he was fit for the job. Then she also told them that he is gay and loves Jesus. Long story short, although he was the only one to apply for this role, they said they couldn't give him an interview because of his sexuality.

What happened next is one of the many moments I realized that my wife is a total badass. Remember how I felt caught in an endless loop? Sami felt stuck too, but for some reason, when this community of people we loved said they wouldn't even bring Brian in for an interview, she snapped. It's like someone shook her, and she woke up. She marched into our boss's office and said, "You have one week to change your mind about Brian or I'm gone." Cue "Eye of the Tiger" set to every step as she dropped the mic and walked out of his office. She knew they weren't going to change their minds, but giving them a week just added dramatic effect. (She is a queen, and I love it.) Of course, a week went by, and in that week Sami found another job at a place called The Giving Keys. It was a really cool jewelry company with an incredible mission. The office was in the arts district in Los Angeles, and you didn't have to be a Christian to work there. It was perfect. When our boss said the answer was no, Sami was gone in a blaze of integrity and glory.

In the many moments and conversations during that week, I asked Sami, "What clicked?" I was scared shitless because Sami had gotten out of the endless loop but I was still in it, and I had no idea what that meant for us. Sami told me that the only difference between us and Brian was that he was living in freedom and we were living in secret. She said she realized she did not want to be a part of a place that rewarded secrets but not freedom. So she left. She started this new job and instantly made a million friends because that's just who she is. Wouldn't you know it—not a single one of those friends cared that she was gay. Her boss didn't care, her boss's boss didn't care, her job wasn't in question, and she was living free. The only bummer? I was not. I was not free but Sami was, so there came a point when she had to let me go. She tried dragging me out of the loop with her, but my white knuckles gripped the inside of the closet too tightly. I was truly stuck. If you have ever been in a fear spiral, you know how hard it can be to get out.

In the wake of feeling like I had lost Sami, feeling like the community I had wasn't real because it wasn't honest, I got to a level of sadness that my optimistic enneagram seven heart had never felt before. Have you ever been so sad you think maybe you will always be sad? I was still stuck in the fear spiral. I had stayed so long that I had actually lost both of the things I was afraid of losing. I started seriously resenting every moment I was at work, and the rest of the time I was just devastated about losing Sami. I knew the only way to even have a shot at what I wanted and the freedom that was waiting for me was to just freaking do it. I had to face the fear, choose the freedom, quit the job, come out, and get the love of my life back. I knew what to do, but I didn't know how.

Luckily, this was right around the time that I was turning thirty—because sometimes it's helpful to be going through identity crisis and then add a milestone birthday on top of that. Anyone else love doubling down on an identity crisis?

Alone in my apartment one night—where I lived by myself, no other humans, and just one dog—I finally shook myself out of my fear loop. On one of the walls of my apartment was a poster: a blown-up photograph of now-Congressman John Lewis and Dr. Martin Luther King Jr. leading the 1965 march for voting rights in Selma, Alabama. The year before, I had the opportunity to take a group of people on a civil rights tour, visiting places like Jackson, Mississippi, Selma, Alabama, and Birmingham, Alabama. We went all over the South, visited historic sights, interviewed people who were a part of the movement, and ended the trip in Washington, DC talking about future change for our country. The trip was wonderful, and when we were in Selma, there was a man on the bridge selling these posters, so we all bought one.

When we got to DC at the end of our trip, we were privileged to have an interview with John Lewis to talk about his role in the civil rights movement, his speech at the march on Washington, and his work now. There were only ten of us in the room with him, and at the end of our time, we asked him if he would sign the posters that we bought in Selma, since he was the man front and center of all of them. He agreed, and that poster, framed in my apartment, was one of my truly most prized possessions. That night in my apartment, I found myself just staring at that poster, and then I found myself staring in the mirror. I would look at the poster and look in the mirror and look at the poster and look in the mirror. At one point I looked at the poster and audibly asked, "How did you do it?" I truly wanted to know. The people on the bridge that day had both everything to lose and everything to gain. They believed so deeply in the freedom that they wanted, believed that they deserved that freedom. They believed so much that they came back to that bridge three times before the march was successful. How did they do it?

I kept looking at the poster and back at myself until I realized something that finally shook me out of the loop. I looked at the poster and back at myself and reminded myself that I have that strength. Those are my people, my community, and my ancestors; that blood runs in my veins. I come from a long history of people who stood up against all odds to claim the freedom they deserved—a freedom that was real and worth fighting for. I looked at that poster and saw myself, my kids, and their kids. I looked at that picture and back at myself and finally felt the strength I had hoped was in me all along.

I know choosing freedom is hard, but there is so much strength inside of us and all around us. When I think about what my ancestors in Mississippi would think of my life now and the legacy I want to leave for my kids and theirs, I remember that **strength is inherited. We don't have to do things alone.** We do not exist in a vacuum. I had to borrow strength from John Lewis and Bayard Rustin and Fannie Lou Hamer. I had to borrow strength from my parents and from Sami. It's okay to look at yourself in the mirror sometimes and remind yourself who the fuck you are. Actually, it's not just okay—it's necessary. If you look in the mirror and don't see strength, then grab a picture of someone you see strength in and borrow theirs until you can see it in yourself.

Choosing freedom and shaking yourself out of a fear loop is hard work. It doesn't always come naturally, but it just might be one of the things most worth fighting for. I am grateful for those who came before me. I am grateful for my fight, and I hope everyone after me keeps fighting. I hope you reading this find your fight. There is always room for more freedom. We always need it.

I quit my job the next week. I called Sami and told her I wanted nothing else more in the world than to be with her. If that meant giving up my role as a pastor, losing that community, and finding a new job, then I would do it. It was not only because she is the most amazing woman in the world but also because it was finally time for me to embrace freedom. Choosing Sami over everything else represented me finally getting out of the fear spiral. She is my act of resistance, and I am so happy she was willing to welcome me out of the loop with open arms.

Was everything magical and perfect from that moment on? Wouldn't it be nice if that's how it worked? After I left my job as a pastor at a megachurch, I really wasn't sure what to do next. What do you do after you leave a job with seemingly no transferable skills on paper? "Hi, I was a pastor at a megachurch. I think I am qualified to run your tech company" is a sentence that does not come out of people's mouths. I eventually ended up finding a job in the African American resource center at the local public college. Was it a good job? Yes. Did it pay in real dollars? Yes. Did I cry basically every day on my way to and from there? Also yes. I didn't leave my church job and fall into my dream life. And while I loved the students I worked with, my job in the resource center involved processing so much trauma and confusion that sometimes I would just close the door and whisper, "What the fuck?" to myself until it was time to go home.

My life with Sami was so wonderful, and everything else felt like a shitstorm. Who was I if I wasn't a pastor? What was I going to do? What were my goals? Where could I go? I will never forget driving home from work one day, calling my friend Rachel, and asking her, "Do you know anything about pharmaceutical sales? Do you think that's what I should do?"

Every day felt like a different grab at an idea that might be worth trying. Luckily, I had good friends who reminded me that pharmaceutical sales, sports management, and maybe was I supposed to be a rapper—were all bad ideas. I needed to just keep moving forward and digging deep into what was happening internally and what I really wanted. Everything felt so confusing, and even though it was gut-wrenchingly hard to live with so much uncertainty, I knew it was better than sitting in meetings and hearing people say how wrong it was to be me. No, this season of my life was not marked by magical amounts of clarity and success. It was so freaking hard, but it was honest. I knew that just because it was hard it didn't mean it was wrong, and I knew this was the kind of hard that was going to create something beautiful in me. Honestly, as strange as it may sound, crying in my car on the hour-long drive every day to and from that job was some of the most free moments of my life up until that point.

Don't fall for the lie that the easy thing to do is also the right thing to do. Sometimes it's the hard roads that take us to where we need to go. Sometimes it's crying in the car that reminds us how strong we are. So do the scary thing. It will probably be hard, but I promise you are strong enough—and if you don't think you are, then borrow someone else's strength until you believe it. We need more people in this world to get out of the fear loop and start living a life that is real.

7

WE NEED
EACH OTHER

Out of the nine tattoos on my body, four of them are matching tattoos that I got with other people. You could say that matching tattoos are my love language. My wife and I both have tattoos that say, "Stay awake" as a reminder to stay present and do our best to not miss all of the incredible moments around us every day. My two best friends from college and I all have roman numeral III on our sides because, well, there's three of us. My wife and I have two best friends, Marx and Paul. They are also a couple, they are also gay, and so yeah, we all got matching rainbow tattoos one day. Last but not least, my wife and I also have matching tattoos with our friend Rachel. The three of us have the number nineteen on our wrists. The story behind this tattoo reminds me every day why choosing freedom is difficult, worth it, and extremely vulnerable.

I had been friends with Rachel for about a year or two before I told her about me and Sami, but she already knew, or at least she strongly suspected. Right in the beginning of my friendship with Rachel (which was also the middle of the "oh my God I'm gay" shitstorm), I decided to run a half marathon, and Rachel, being a big running advocate and amazing friend, drove me from LA to San Francisco to run the race. On the way home, we were driving through the middle of nowhere California. We had run through what I thought were all possible conversation topics, and then after a slight pause, she said, "Sami is gay, right?"

I literally froze. How did she know! (To be fair I think the better question is how did people *not* know. We wore matching Birkenstocks and took all of our vacations together.) But I did not know what to do, and I just blurted out, "Um no, hmmmm, maybe. Not that I know of. Probably not."

I think I was awkward enough for Rachel to leave it alone for the time being. But ever since I met her and certainly after that conversation, she was very high on my list of people I was pretty sure would support us if we gave her the opportunity, and damn was I right. We initially met Rachel because we all went to the same church—the church where I was a pastor and Sami ran marketing and production and had a hand in most of the creative output of the church. Rachel and her whole family were some of the many people who found that church and instantly felt like they were at home, that this was the church they had been looking for their whole lives.

It had so very much to offer. It was extremely racially and ethnically diverse (for a church), and we didn't shy away from hard conversations about race. Women were represented in leadership roles, which felt like a huge win at the time. It was very well organized and full of talented people, so everything—from music to sermons to lights—was all run to near perfection. So yeah, of course Rachel and her family loved the church and the people as much as we did. We had no intention of changing that for her.

Shortly after Sami quit her job, I quit my job. We had gotten back together, and we were ready to figure to what it meant to be free. We knew that meant coming out publicly. We had tiptoed around, telling friends here and there, not sure if we could or even would ever proclaim it to the world. Eventually, we knew we needed to. Not coming out publicly was like the last thread of a fear sweater that had been slowly unraveling for years. It felt like our last stand—or really, our first stand for a new life.

It was one of the greatest feelings in my life to hit "post" on a blog and share cute pictures of the two of us on social media, but the repercussions of that post were far-reaching. So many of our close friends were from church because when you work at a church and go to a church, most of your community comes from that church. Almost all of our friends, coworkers, and neighbors were from that context, so needless to say, we ruffled a few feathers by coming out publicly, not being ashamed of who we are, and proclaiming a message that God still loves us and it is, in fact, 100 percent okay to be gay.

I sat down to talk with each of my old bosses. One of those conversations went *fine,* and one of them went terribly. But overall, I received the message that who *we are* conflicted with what *they believed* and taught and wanted for their church. Okay, whatever. We knew the risk. We knew that we would probably be on the outside of the community that we loved. We were ready and willing to pay that cost. But something else happened that we were less ready for. We were at happy hour with Rachel one day, telling her about these conversations and some of the things that the church leadership said to us—including new policies they were starting because of us. Then she said, "Hold on." She got out her phone, sent a text to her husband, and let him know that they were not going back to that church anymore.

It was wild. I watched her like it was happening in slow motion. After sitting in all of these conversations with people who claimed to love us but couldn't accept us, all of a sudden one of our friends, who we knew *loved* that church dearly, was immediately willing to stand up for us and take that loss with us. Her response changed so many things for us and was validating beyond words.

Rachel later wrote a book (she's written many books because she's a boss) in which she talked about her experience deciding to leave that church and stand with us and everything that meant for her. The publisher tried to remove that chapter because it felt "too controversial," and Rachel fought back. She had to make revisions, but she still got it in the book. After this, we each got 19 tattoos to commemorate what chapter 19 represented for all of us: standing for what is right, for what we believe in, and standing with the people around us we love. And for me, it also sits on my wrist as a permanent reminder that **you are not ever alone in your fight,** and even though it is so hard to face your own fears and your own loss, it is sometimes even harder to watch people who love you face their own fear and their own loss on your behalf. That is some seriously hard and necessary work.

Rachel wasn't the only person in our lives who put us in the uncomfortable position of watching as people who loved us were willing to lose something so we could win. When Sami and I realized that we were in love and were in way over our heads trying to process it all, we started going to therapy. We saw the same therapist, together and separately, for the next few years until we were out and together. Our therapist was like a magician for those years, walking us through some really complex emotional territory. In sessions with her, we would cry and hope and dream. We would tell her everything, and she held it all for us.

Naturally, when it came time for us to get married, we asked her if she would be the one to perform the ceremony, because she was such a significant part of us getting to that day. She said yes, and we all cried. We didn't know much about her personal life, because she was our therapist and that's just the way it is when professionals have good boundaries. But we did know that her husband was a pastor. As we prepped for the wedding, we started to learn more and more about her and her life. As it turned out, we have a ton of mutual friends (which was hilarious to see at our wedding). She married us and said some of the most beautiful words that I will truly never forget. But after that day, after choosing to say yes, she also had to face the reality of fear and loss.

Here's the backstory: the church where her husband was a pastor was actually also the church that he had grown up in. He was incredibly involved in the junior high and high school ministries and went to college for pastoral studies near the church so he could still be a part of the community. When they got married, they actually moved into the house her husband had grown up in near the church. Just to recap, this man had grown up in a house by a church that he went to his whole life. Then he went to college to become a pastor at that same church, where he also got married, and he moved into that same house. His life was set. He had been a pastor there for twelve years when his wife so delightfully agreed to marry us. Because she decided to stand with us, that was his last year as a pastor at that church. The details are his story to tell, but at the end of the day, he was another person who loved us and experienced loss so we could experience more.

Before we came out, my dad was on the board of our church and ran the men's ministry. He had so many friends and such a strong community at that church. But after we came out and my parents chose to stand with us and love us, he lost that community. My mom was the same way. She led mentorship groups, and friends she's had for years fell away when she chose to stand with us.

It's one thing to face your fears, suffer loss, and realize that you were stronger than you ever knew. But it is something entirely different when you are forced to watch others do that on your behalf—for others to experience loss for your gain. I'm not sure I've had a more vulnerable experience in my life, but I know it had to happen. I know how quickly I would do and have done the same for people I love. I know it makes me better every time. But there is nothing more uncomfortable than watching others suffer loss because they love you.

I remember right before we got engaged, famed Christian writer and speaker Jen Hatmaker made a public statement about her position as affirming. People lost their shit. Jen went through hell and back for love. Bookstores pulled her books from the shelf, and people were literally burning her books. She went silent for a while on the internet, and I can only imagine the kinds of messages she was receiving. Of course, Jen Hatmaker had absolutely no idea who Sami and I were. Still, as I watched her go through so much struggle, I knew she believed that it was worth it because of people like us. That's the thing about standing up for someone—you inevitably end up standing for way more people than you thought. So many people were watching Rachel and my dad and our therapist and her husband and Jen Hatmaker. **People notice when you stand up for truth. That doesn't make it any easier, but it does make it that much more important.**

As difficult as that season was as we watched friend after friend and parent after parent be thrown into the ring because we chose to love each other, it has also been one of the most beautiful things to watch. **We have learned how important true community is, and we have learned how good it feels to stand for what you believe in and to watch others stand with you.**

And you know what? Rachel's book ended up doing pretty well. She and her family moved to Austin, and they have found their own freedom in so many ways. Our therapist's husband, the pastor who could no longer be a pastor at his church after twelve years? Well, turns out he had always dreamt of being a firefighter and thought he never could. As I write this book, he is about halfway through fire academy and well on his way to that dream. And my parents? Well, if you ask them, they will say me coming out was one of the best things that ever happened to them. They are awake in a way I haven't seen them be in years, and although it was difficult to see the loss they went through, they are both excited and dreaming about what comes next.

Just because it's hard or even uncomfortable doesn't mean it's bad. The ripples that went out from our decision felt like they went for miles. At times it was so hard not to feel guilty for all the lives that changed because people believed in us. It was hard not to feel responsible for jobs lost and hard conversations with family members and fights with publishers. It was hard to not question our decision because of these things, but the more I think about it, I realize that those ripples were hard and surprising and confusing but so necessary. **Sometimes we need the ripple of someone else's life to shake ours up.** That has certainly happened for me, and I am happy to be that ripple too. It's okay to get uncomfortable, and it's okay to make some ripples and even some waves. **We need to be willing to shake up the still waters, and that's not something we can accomplish alone.**

The list of things that no one should do alone is long and includes everything from swing dancing to putting sunscreen on your back. Change is also one of those things. We need people. We need them desperately for so many parts of our lives. We need them to remind us what is worth fighting for. We need them to remind us how strong we are. We need them to stand with us, and we absolutely need to feel what it's like for someone to stand for us. It is humbling and terrifying, gut-wrenching, and beautiful. We cannot and should not do things alone.

SHED THE
FALSE SELF

Right before I started middle school, my family moved from Southern California to suburban Colorado. Even though this was pre–social media, somehow by my first day, most of the kids at my school already knew I was a new student from California. I'm not going to lie—this really helped my entry into a new school because not only does being a new student make you interesting, but I was also a new student from what most kids understood to be a fun place.

Before we moved, my family and I lived in Whittier, California. It's not a place that's necessarily known for its proximity to the beach—but not one single person at my new school knew that. Apparently they all assumed that every house in Southern California is a beach house in Malibu. I neither confirmed nor denied their instant portrayal of me as a surfer girl who couldn't wait to get back to the water.

At this point in my life (and honestly, still today), I had what I like to describe as a natural aversion to water. I will get in the water, but it's not my favorite. I never get my face wet, and I proudly swim doggy paddle style. But again, none of my new school friends knew any of this, so when the rumors of my near-professional-level surfing abilities spread, I did not stop them. At some point, a part of the rumor got back to me. I realized the story going around the school was that I was such a good surfer that I had a surfing scholarship to UCLA, and that's why I was so mad my parents moved to Colorado. Now, not only does UCLA not have surfing scholarships, but even if they did, I am pretty confident they wouldn't be throwing them out to middle schoolers who can barely swim to save their life. I wasn't even mad about moving to Colorado. It was a great place to live.

But alas, I was in no condition to pass up friends. I had just started a new school, and if I had to let the rumors of my unmatched surfing abilities slide to stay in the good graces of these new tweens, then that's just what I had to do. For full commitment to my new role, I begged my mom to take me to Tilly's so I could buy some clothes that would corroborate my story. Brands like Roxy and Billabong became staples of my wardrobe. It didn't hurt that when the first snow fell that year and all the kids went sledding, I didn't have a sled because we had just moved, but we did have an old boogie board in the garage and I used that. This was the cherry on top that sealed my new identity.

Eventually the rumors of my unmatched surfing abilities died off without me ever having to explain to my classmates that I can barely swim. But unfortunately, the practice of taking on a false self to meet others' expectations was not a phenomenon that ended when I graduated from the eighth grade. Sure, the circumstances have been different, and since then I haven't let rumors of me being any sort of professional athlete spread. But there have been other ways in my life that I have let other people's assumptions and expectations lead me to create an inauthentic and false version of myself. I think I'm safe to assume that I am not the only one who has ever experienced that. We all know what it feels like when we allow other people's standards, expectations, and even assumptions of who we are control us. We inevitably create a false self. This is the self that doesn't become who we want to be—or even show who we actually are. This is the self that only shows what people want to see. This self meets the necessary qualifications for entry to an exclusive club but denies who we really are to fit in. Honestly, this is the self that is happy to sign the purity pledge at the youth retreat every year even though you have actually been having sex since you were nineteen (and enjoying it, for that matter).

We do these things all because of the fear of being honest. Or more accurately, it is the fear that honesty will put us out of the good graces of the new friends at our school or the leaders in our churches. So we sign a card because everyone else is signing a card. That is our false self. It is the false self I know a lot of women in particular have created—the self that is pretending that your feet haven't been hurting since 1998 wearing shoes that no human being should be forced to wear, simply because heels are the standard for "what women should wear." (Okay, this one was more personal because I've never been able to walk in heels. I look like a baby deer when I try. My sister was made for them, and I have literally seen her break into a light jog in a pair of stilettos, so tomato, to-mah-to on this one.) **We create false selves around expectations that do not even serve us.**

When we create a false self and that self begins to conflict with our true self, we have what is called an identity crisis. When I worked in a nonaffirming church and I was desperately in love with a woman, I had to shed the false self I had created to fit into that space. I had to stop making weird jokes about guys that I thought were "hot," and I had to stop pretending to listen when coworkers would talk about the friends that they wanted to set me up with. I had to let that go and lean into the true self—who I wanted to be and was meant to be. Pretending to be someone I wasn't simply to appease the people around me was not a sustainable way to live.

I believe to this day that identity crisis saved my life. Finally allowing myself to pull back the layers of that false self and begin to embrace who I truly am is probably one if the single best things that has ever happened to me. Even today, I catch myself every now and then still feeling so happy and free when I am in a group of people and we are talking about our favorite shows or celebrities we think are hot. (Yes, I know this is a bit objectifying, but we are only human.) Now I get to be truly me in those conversations, honestly responding that Emilia Clarke (Daenerys Targaryen from *Game of Thrones*) is, in my mind, an archetype of what it means to be a "hot" celebrity. Gone are the days I have pretended to be attracted to Brad Pitt just because I knew that was an acceptable answer. (Just as a side note here, I feel the need to share with you all how bad my wife was at pretending she wasn't gay. Whenever she was asked about her celebrity crush, she would always say Morgan Freeman. Now, not that Morgan Freeman is not handsome and wonderful, but it was a strange answer for a twenty-five-year-old girl from Orange County.) But no matter the topic, feeling congruent in what I say and what I actually believe has brought a peace that runs so deep it is hard to even explain.

Our experiences have taught us that our false self is easier to shed when we are talking about superficial things. Sami and I have two friends we hang out with more than anyone else. They are our constants, and we make sure to spend time with them every week—more than once a week if we are lucky. Their names are Marx and Paul, and we are obsessed.

But we have not always been this close, and there was a time when we were first becoming friends where things still felt new and fragile. For the first few meals we shared together, Sami and I invited them to come eat with us at our favorite sushi restaurant. We probably ate there together ten times. It was a great little tradition we were starting. But as we became closer friends and started feeling more and more comfortable around each other, Paul finally told us that he hates sushi. He sat there and watched us eat sushi and pretended to be happy about it for months! Now that he's been able to shed some of his false self around us, he could be honest about how much he hates sushi, and the four of us have not gone to sushi together since. Although this example probably went on a little long, shedding your false self when it comes to superficial things like food preference or movie preference or finally being able to speak your mind when someone asks you, "What do you want to eat?" is difficult, but not impossible. The hardest work comes when we need to shed the false self that is tied to our worth, our belief, and the people around us.

Shedding the false self and being able to accept, value, and live into your true self is extremely difficult. I often wonder which is worse: people not knowing the real me or people knowing the real me but not accepting me. The two feel equally painful. Our friend Brian says that when he was living into his false self, he felt like he was never able to truly feel loved because even though people said they loved him, they only loved his false self, and that didn't feel real. You don't have to be in the closet to know what Brian is talking about. It truly is terrifying to think that if people knew our real selves, they might not love us anymore.

This cycle is endless, and neither option is easy. But only one option allows you to shed your false self. Only one option allows you to know *for sure* that when someone says, "I love you," they are talking about the real you. That feeling is worth one thousand affirmations of our false self.

Our friend Paul, feeling a new sense of freedom after he told us he hates sushi, is currently in his own identity evolution. Paul was a worship pastor at a megachurch for ten years. Actually, even though we recently became close friends, I have known who he is since college because he was basically a worship leader god at our small, private Christian college until he made it to the big leagues of the megachurch world. So much of his identity was tied to that world. I have since come to love Paul very deeply as he is one of my best friends. Among the many things I love about Paul is that he is the kind of person who you can always count on. If he says he will be somewhere or do something, he absolutely will. He is so smart. He is an incredible musician and is kind and sweet and funny and takes his responsibilities in the world very seriously. He also makes incredible bread. I wish deeply that I could give everyone who reads this a loaf of his bread, but that's beside the point. Paul is also gay, and like most people who grew up in the church, he had no framework for reconciling his faith and his sexuality. Paul could have existed in the church world for a long time if he had never shed his false self. But a few years ago, Paul decided to face the fear of being outside the only community he had ever known and chose to shed his false self. He came out, found his way outside of the church world, and had an experience unlike anything he had experienced when his life was led by his false self.

But here's the thing about shedding the false self and about change and growing—it's not something that we only do once.

Coming out was one thing, but then Paul found his person, and they started dating. Suddenly, Paul found himself in another season of showing his true self—this time as someone who is in love. The truth is, each time we reveal another layer of our true selves, we have to deal with what that means for the people we love and the people around us. Paul's new relationship seemingly started the cycle all over again. Whether spoken or unspoken, I think a lot of his close family and friends were able to accept Paul's sexuality if he remained single, but another evolutionary jump was now required all around.

None of this is easy. Each new step into our true selves is a new level of vulnerability and a true reminder of just how hard facing your fears is. It is terrifying to think that the people who have loved you might only be able to love your false self. Not everyone is going to come with you as you move forward in your life. But at the end of the day, the choice is yours. You can stop being who you are, stop moving forward in your life, stop pursuing love so you can keep people and circumstances in your life the same, or you can shed that false self but know that everyone might not feel the same about who you really are. Both are hard, but one is free.

It has been one of the greatest lessons in my life to learn that just because something is hard doesn't mean that it's bad. I used to think that any and all conflict or friction was a negative thing, but you know what? **We need friction and resistance to build strength. Just because it's hard and it sucks does not mean it's wrong. It means you're getting stronger.**

I have stopped asking myself what the easiest way out of things is (a bad habit I picked up in my teens). Instead I have started asking myself which road leads to more freedom. Which path is worth the work? Who will I become after I take this step? Life is not about avoiding pain. It's not about creating false selves so we experience less friction. It's about choosing to grow even when it's hard. So those parts of you that you keep hidden because you're afraid will cause friction? The parts of your story that you keep secret because they might make things hard? It's time to let them out. **Shed your false self, create the friction, embrace the hard work, and watch who you will become in the process.**

The thing is, we don't just have one false self in our lives. Shedding the false self is ongoing. My friend Paul had to tell us he didn't like sushi. He had to come out, and then he had to tell people about his relationship. And that was all in just two years. I can't imagine in his life or mine how many more times a false self will need to be shed. Shedding the false self is not a one-time event; it's a process.

I think one of the easiest ways to know if there is a false self that you need to shed is to ask yourself whether there is a question you desperately hope someone will ask you. I had a friend who was married at age twenty-one to a woman and later realized that he was gay. For as long as he knew this and was still married to her, he desperately hoped and wished she would just ask him so he could finally tell her. I have another friend who has had a long experience with abusing alcohol, and she said in her early days of drinking heavily, she was desperately waiting for someone to notice and ask her if she had a problem so she could address it.

When I was a pastor at a megachurch, I remember thinking to myself, *If my boss would ever just straight up ask me if*

I wanted to be here, then I could say no, and that would be my way out. We all know the feeling of wanting to be asked a question so badly. If there is a question you are desperately waiting for someone to ask you, you can shed your false self by not waiting for anyone to ask you the question. **Just start living the answer.**

9 CHANGE IS NOT ALWAYS GOING TO FEEL GOOD

I have a habit of working out one time and assuming that I will instantly become Serena Williams. I leave one SoulCycle class and I'm like, "I am ready for the Olympics. Where are my sponsorships?"

But the obvious reality is that after one moderate to hard workout, I am only marginally stronger than before. We all know this simple truth: it takes time and resistance to build physical strength. If your goal is to get physically stronger, you will view resistance as a good thing. For whatever reason, though, that message does not translate as well to other areas of life. I grew up thinking that if something was emotionally hard, then maybe it wasn't good. At some point, I inherited a narrative that told me if I was doing the right things then it should be easy and feel good. Because of this idea, I found myself taking the path of least resistance whenever it was available because I thought it was the right thing to do. For everything from simple, small decisions to bigger, more substantial ones, I tried my best to avoid tension and conflict because those things were hard, and in my understanding, hard meant bad.

I began my freshman year of college as a proud philosophy major. I got really into philosophy in high school (nerd alert), and I just knew it was the right major for me. But for my first intro to psychology class my freshman year of college, I had the worst professor. Looking back, I don't think he was a bad person and didn't care about his job. But he was a young adjunct professor with a few other jobs and I am going to assume that we did not get the best of who he was. Now that I am early in my career, I realize that there is a completely new level of tired that you reach after a long day of work, and if, after I finished one job, I had to go teach introductory philosophy to a bunch of college freshmen, I probably would be about as present as he was. This negative experience with this one professor in this one class led me to change my major to something that felt more right: psychology. I ended up sticking with it and getting a bachelors and master's in psychology. I don't regret it at all, but changing my major after one conflicting experience with a professor is just one of many examples of how I avoided tension. Rather than addressing that professor or having a conversation with my academic advisor or literally taking any actions to stay in that conversation, I just dropped it and ran the other way. I would rather have changed my major than have a hard conversation with someone. That same impulse to avoid difficulty shows up all over my life.

This idea of things being good if they were easy followed me into friendships. If a friendship felt difficult or tense or uncomfortable, I would interpret it as "not meant to be." I look back on some of my past friendships and realize I was the person who was desperately avoiding asking the questions that my friends so desperately needed to be asked.

I remember when one of my best friends started drinking to the point that it felt like a problem. Often by the time I got to her house, she would already be drunk, and then she would want to go out drinking and would be blacked out by the end of the night. This was her routine. There was a part of me that *knew* I had to address it and bring up a potentially very difficult conversation, but I just didn't know how. Tension and conflict made me so uncomfortable at that point in my life that instead of being a true friend and addressing the harmful behavior, I enabled it. Eventually, less conflict-averse people in her life confronted her about it, and she went to rehab and has been sober for almost five years now. But I honestly used to think there were just different kinds of people—the people you bring in when something needs to be addressed and the people you bring in when you want to have fun. I was a fun person, not a serious person who brought up hard things.

Any other "fun" people out there?

Well, being the fun person is all fun and games until you realize you have stayed in your church job that won't let you be who you are for far too long because you are afraid of the conflict and tension it will cause. Or you are the fun person who stayed in the closet so long because the tension you felt with your sexuality made you believe it was bad. Or you are the fun person who can't seem to shed your false self because you're afraid people won't like your true self. Not only was I unable to ask my friends the hard questions, but I also wasn't able to ask myself them either. That is actually not fun.

I was in SoulCycle a couple of weeks ago, and my friend Chris was teaching the class. If you've never been to Soul-Cycle, it's a spin class that essentially serves three purposes: it's a workout, it's also like going to the club, and then there are also moments where it feels like therapy. In SoulCycle, like any other spin class, you are literally riding a bike that's not going anywhere and are wearing these special shoes that clip into the pedals. There is a little knob on your bike just below the handlebars, and if you turn that knob to the right, things get a lot harder, and if you turn it to the left, smooth sailing.

We were in this class and pedaling our little hearts out, and Chris was talking to us on his Britney Spears wraparound microphone. We had been turning that little knob to the right and adding so much resistance on our bikes, and it felt like we were pedaling through mud. The music was pumping us up, and Chris was pumping us up. Finally, I thought we were done adding resistance. I was ready for some left turns, if you know what I mean. My legs felt like they were going to fall off because, as I mentioned earlier, working out one time every few weeks does not produce Serena Williams results. But then Chris started to prepare us for another big push. He told us that we were the only ones who could reach down and turn the knob. We were the only ones in our lives who could add the resistance we needed to get stronger. I actually hate how cliché it sounds, but it is *so true* that resistance builds strength. That is really the only way. And we are the ones responsible for adding that resistance. We are the ones who get to decide that we are going to move through it. We can choose to push ourselves, or we can pretend we didn't hear the world around us telling us to add more resistance. You can live a life that always tries to turn the little knob to the left, but if you do that, I can promise that you will not get any stronger than you are today. Hard things are the only way. Have you ever heard someone say, "Everything in my life is so good and easy right now, and I am growing a ton because of it"?

Instead of avoiding the things that may feel uncomfortable in our lives, we need to walk toward them, take them straight on, and accept that resistance only makes us stronger. You can't get strong without resistance and resistance rarely feels good, but what lies on the other side of it is what makes up the beautiful parts of life. I know I am already on the edge of using too many quotes from fitness instructors, but honestly, I have been so inspired lately by people who understand what it physically takes to get strong because I think it has the potential to teach us a lot about what it takes to become emotionally strong.

I was in a different spin class the other day, and the instructor, as she was encouraging us to keep pushing even though it was uncomfortable and we were sweating our asses off, said this: "The pride you will feel for making it through this uncomfortable moment will last longer than this discomfort." I couldn't agree more. I am not going to tell you there is a magic formula for your life that will make it not hard. Moving through hard things is so very uncomfortable, *but* the pride of moving through them lasts so much longer than that discomfort.

It's not going to feel amazing all the time and it's going to get scary and heavy, but we have to do it anyway.

My wife always says that if she knew what was waiting for her on the other side, she would have sprinted out of the closet a long time ago. And what was waiting for her on the other side was not all sunshine and daisies and rainbows. It wasn't a life void of uncomfortable feelings or hard things. It was freedom. It was the chance to be fully honest and fully known and the chance to be loved as all of who she was.

A mentor in college told me something that has stuck with me and has guided every season of my life since. She told me, "You can only experience joy to the depth at which you are willing to experience pain because they come from the same well." If we close ourselves off to pain, then we close ourselves off to joy too. If we close ourselves off to resistance, then we close ourselves off to strength. **If we close ourselves off from anything that's hard, we close ourselves off from the opportunity to grow.**

I wish this wasn't true. I wish you could have massive, expanding joy without ever experiencing any pain, but you just can't. Have you ever experienced a season or a moment in time when you were so sad you thought you would never laugh again? And then do you remember your first laugh after that? The first laugh after the deepest sadness comes from a deeper place now because the whole well has expanded.

I want to pause here to just make something clear: **not all pain is productive.** We don't have to stick with pain that is caused by abuse. That kind of pain will only bring more pain, not growth. You do not have to wait around to find the redemptive side of an abusive relationship. Boundaries are real, they are necessary, and you have every right to claim safety for yourself. Please do not hear me say that all pain is good and we should stick around for it. Some pain does not serve you, and I am advocating that we know the difference between the two.

My grandmother passed away twelve years ago. My mom is one of *ten* children, and my grandmother was the matriarch of our expansive and consistently growing, big, loud, Mexican family. When she passed away, the void in all of our worlds felt too massive to ever be repaired. I was so sad and wondered what would ever bring joy again or whether this big, loud family would ever be together laughing again. I remember standing at the cemetery when the ceremony was over, after my sweet, angelic grandmother had been lowered into the ground. All of the sudden, one of my little cousins, who was there at the cemetery playing with cars behind all of the adults, saw his opportunity. While all of us were crying and consoling one another, he snuck up to the front, and just as we all realized what was happening, it was too late. My little cousin took the plastic monster truck that he was playing with, and with what seemed like the shooting ability of Michael Jordan with perfect form, he shot the truck down into the grave they had just moments before lowered my grandmother into.

After the shocking silence of waiting for the truck to fall, a few seconds later we heard three loud *thuds* as the truck bounced around and finally landed. Everyone stood silent for a moment, and then a laugh bellowed out of me from a deeper place than a laugh had ever come from. I remember looking over at my family members as we all laughed with tears in our eyes. We were still so hurt and still mourning and in pain, but we also felt this hilarious joy that my cousin had so uniquely delivered. That's the thing—our joy and laughter did not minimize our pain, and our mourning and pain did not have to stop us from experiencing joy. Those are imaginary lines that we have drawn, and we need to learn to erase them if we want to be able to do hard things well.

Sometimes we want to put our life experiences in a box or create categories for those experiences, like good or bad, happy or sad, but the truth is that most of our meaningful life experiences are both happy and sad, both challenging and gratifying. I think about my journey of coming out. Even though I would do it again one million times because of the life I have now, it was so hard and so painful, and I faced so much resistance and tension. But it was also so beautiful and wonderful. If joy and pain truly come from the same well, then coming out looks like just taking the lid off the whole thing—all the pain and all the joy at once. This is what it means to truly be present—walking into the hard things knowing they will not be void of joy and walking into the joyful things knowing they will not be void of pain.

That's the thing about facing fear—it will be hard, but that doesn't mean it will be void of good. Hard doesn't mean bad. Yes, facing our fears will be scary, and yes, it may be painful and it might suck—a lot—but I promise you it's worth it.

Several years ago I went to a conference where Glennon Doyle gave a keynote speech. She said it was the biggest audience she had spoken to, so she was nervous but vulnerable and amazing. She spoke about her then very new book *Carry On, Warrior,* which had become wildly successful and had earned the early title of *New York Times* bestseller. She talked about how difficult it was to find time and space to write while raising her children and having a life. She even went so far as to write in the closet in her bedroom and all sorts of other strange places just to get it done.

Then she said something that has stuck with me ever since. She said that she imagined it would have been a whole lot easier to write the book if she knew the outcome. If she knew that the book was going to be a *New York Times* bestseller and change her life and her family's life, if she knew the trajectory that this book would set her life on or the opportunities it would open up, then she would have just jumped right up and written it! But then she said that's not why you write books. Or at least she said that's not why she wrote her book. It's not about doing something because you know the outcome; it's about doing something because you feel called to do it. **Sometimes you just have to do the thing because you know it's the thing you need to do, not because it will be easy or successful but because it will be true.**

The reality is that most of the truly meaningful and memorable moments in our lives aren't the easiest ones. The things we choose to sacrifice for—the painful moments, telling the truth, writing the book, asking for forgiveness, and calling the therapist—these moments have the opportunity to make the biggest impact in our lives, but they aren't the moments where we get to hit the easy button and they cost us nothing. It's the moments that are hard, the moments when we want to turn back, the moments when our palms are sweaty and our hearts are racing—those are the moments that define us. Facing our fears, finding joy, growing, evolving—all of it will be hard, but we have to do it anyway. There is no easy way, and we are often faced with two hard options: give into fear and negativity and refuse to be true to who we are, or be true to who we are and pay the price for going outside of what is expected of us. Both are hard, but one is worth it. Just because it's not easy doesn't mean it's not good. Just do the thing.

10 FEAR IS AN OPPRESSOR

When I made the decision to leave my job, leave the confines of the church, and change my life in the best way and choose love, I was still riddled with fear. When Sami and I left our church jobs, we were both free from the narratives that told us we couldn't be who we were or be together or that our love was bad. But even though those voices and that narrative were no longer around us, I began to notice they still had power over us. In the very first few months of being free, we still didn't really tell anybody. I was still afraid to hold her hand or kiss her in public. Instead of making some sort of big public declaration, we just decided to let people find out on their own. Fear still had a real grip on us.

On our very first official date after neither of us worked for a church and we weren't afraid of losing our jobs, we went to a concert in downtown LA. It was so exciting to be on a date with her and imagine doing all of the things you do with your girlfriend at a concert: hold hands and dance together and kiss her on the cheek just because. I was so ready to see what life was like on the other side because I had literally spent three years in a reality where going on a date in public with Sami was my biggest dream in life. I will never forget the feelings of waiting in line at the venue and holding hands and flirting. It was magical. It felt like a grown-up version of a first date in middle school. It was way less awkward but just as exciting.

As we walked into the venue, trying to find our seats, and as I had my arms wrapped around Sami's waist as we made our way through the herds of people, we ran into about ten people from our old church. Cue the saddest music you can think of. Next we ran into another girl from church who was in a small group I led. If that wasn't enough, we kept walking to our seats and ran into a guy and his girlfriend who I used to work with at a very conservative Christian college. Even as I write these words, my stomach still turns with the memory of us almost immediately letting go of each other's hands and dropping my arms from around her waist because fear had trained us so well to be ashamed of who we are. The thing I wanted most and was so excited to have, I gave up in one instant because fear still had a grip on me.

That night was so fun but also so terribly hard for me. Was that how things were always going to be? Would I always be holding Sami's hand loosely so I could let it go fast enough if fear and shame whispered my name? I felt like I had done so much work to get to where I was, but that night showed me that I had more work to do for fear to release its grip on me. Have you ever felt that? Have you ever worked endlessly for the thing you wanted most in life, and then when you got it, you felt like you had to hold it loosely?

After the concert, I started having conversations with Sami about the possibility of doing the thing I was most afraid of at the time: telling everyone on the internet that I was gay. I knew this would open us up to all the criticism in the world, and while it was nice that only our immediate circles knew, it also meant that running into anyone outside of that circle would throw me back into a shame storm. I didn't want to live my life wondering when I might run into the kids of my dad's coworker and have to explain the whole thing to them. I was so tired of being scared that I felt like if I could take on all the fear at once, prove to myself that I was strong enough to do it, and open the floodgates once and for all, then I could be free.

We were both terrified. By the time I left my church job, I had interacted with more than five thousand members of the church, which meant there were more than five thousand potential judgments awaiting me. Even before I was a pastor,

I have always described my life as living on a mountaintop. I have always had a life that people can see and that people have watched, from growing up as a pastor's kid to taking every leadership position possible in college. Now as a pastor, I always took it as a joy and as a responsibility to live a life that others could see. You can imagine that the fear that was allowed to thrive in secret now clung to me in my search for freedom.

Finally, it was the middle of summer, and we decided we were going to rip the Band-Aid off. I had started blogging just to see what would come of it and we both had a decent presence on social media, so I decided to write a blog about my journey, which we would post on the Fourth of July and create our own little independence day. Funny enough, we got a little scared and eventually posted it on the fifth, but the imagery is still there. We made a list of people we wanted to tell in person before they found out on the internet (coming out is such a strange thing). And on July 5, we opened the floodgates. That blog post is still to this day one of the most special things I have ever written and also one of the things that still rings the truest. Here is what it said:

> So this is a post about love, friendship, relationships, and fear. This is a post about how we all stumble across truth in our lives and the real difficulty that comes when we are faced with the opportunity to

stand in it or negotiate with fear. This is a post about the reality of wanting to be light and live in the light and the sacrifices that can come with that. Yes, this is a post about love.

This is also a post about a girl I met a few years ago. Do you ever meet someone, hang out once, and then decide in your head that you are going to be best friends with that person? Me too. So we became best friends. I started learning so much from her, laughing so hard with her, dreaming with her, creating with her, and it was beyond wonderful. This best friendship eventually came to the place where we were both willing to acknowledge that there could be more. We wanted more. More could be beautiful.

We talked and dreamed and imagined what life could be like with more. We talked about the great things that our lives could accomplish together, and we talked about all of the seemingly terrible things we would endure. But in the end, we decided that more was worth it.

I was and still am grateful for a lot of things throughout this journey with her. I am grateful that my relationship with God has only grown stronger since I have known her. I am grateful that I was already deeply rooted in a community that would be as loving and kind and excited as ever when they found out. I am grateful for a family that puts love above everything else. But I was also weirdly grateful for an opportunity to look fear in the face and see what I was actually made of. I was and am grateful that my journey with her has really shown me so much of who I am and who I could be. Am I a person who will shrink down in the face of fear? Will I negotiate my truth? Am I strong enough to stand?

I know that our story will not come without its challenges, and the more people who know, the more challenges will come I am sure. But I was listening to a friend's podcast the other day, and he was talking about how every time he shared his story, he felt a beam of light come into his life. So while telling anyone that will read this on the internet is scary and opens us up to a myriad of criticism, this is also me being flooded with light.

I heard someone say once that fear is a liar. Well, I don't know if that is necessarily true. I think fear is more of an oppressor than a liar. It was fear telling me not to say anything because people might think a certain way about my parents or they might judge or question my relationship with God. It was fear telling me that this might change the way people treat me or my family, and you know what? All of these things are probably true. Fear is not a liar but a captor. Yes, all of those things might very well happen, and now I have a choice to live the rest of my life based on what fear says *or* face fear head-on and remove all of its power. I choose the second.

I am here to say that fear has no power over love, and I will not walk in darkness or bring anyone down there with me.

This post isn't just about me telling everyone that I am super happy to have found someone who is hilarious and brilliant and kind and loves Jesus (although I am). This is a post to say I know I am not the only one who has a choice to make right now—a choice to stand in the light of truth and your story or let the voice of fear shrink you down into darkness. The choice is all of ours.

Let's start standing up to fear in a way that creates freedom for others to stand with us. The world desperately needs us to.

Oh, and Sami, thanks for teaching me one of the greatest things I've ever learned and being there every step of the way as I learned it.

XX,

Brit Barron

In writing that post, I really got in touch with something I still believe with my whole heart today: **fear does not lie to us as much as it keeps us captive.** There is a heaviness to fear that is hard to shake and seemingly can only be faced head-on. I knew what it felt like to take little cracks at the monster but still drop my girlfriend's hand when I got scared. I knew what it felt like to imagine our wedding day or starting a family and be interrupted by thoughts of, "But what would *they* think?" How many times have you thought that? I want to write a book. I want to start that business. I want to move out of the country. I want to pursue music. The list goes on and on. So many of us have said these dreams and then before we even realize it happened, the very next thought in our minds is, *But what would they think?* These thoughts and people and fear held me captive, and I know I am not the only one.

The freedom we are all uniquely called to is standing behind an oppressor that has in some cases become the loudest voice in our head. I love what my friend Brian says about sharing his story. He visualizes his story as a beam of light bursting into the darkness. I know it may sound cliché or trite, but **sharing our story and speaking truth takes the power out of fear.** Your story is what we need to expand the idea of what can be possible. The oppressive narratives of fear intend to make all the stories smaller. That oppressive voice has told us a story about men and women and the very specific roles we need to fill in society. That oppressive voice has told us stories about what a family looks like and convinced us that a family that looks anything other than "normal" is bad. That oppressive voice has told church leaders to make the story of God so small that it doesn't challenge the very nature and the system of church. And that oppressive voice of fear is whispering something to you about why you can't share your story. But let me assure you, **hiding only allows fear to tighten its grip.**

Sometimes the most powerful thing we can do to confront fear is simply to speak. Freedom is the opposite of fear because fear is oppression. Fear keeps us bound and keeps us small. Freedom says, "Go, grow as big as you can, and go as far as you can. Tell as many stories as you can, and never be afraid that you will outgrow goodness."

I often ask myself why it is that the church has become gripped with so much fear, even though Jesus is a figure that has expanded that narrative of freedom and pushed all the boundaries of who was invited to that freedom. How can an organization that is based on his message be so afraid? I have heard people argue over what translation of the Bible can save you and what kind of music gets you closest to God. I have been in countless ridiculous meetings asking and arguing whether woman can be senior pastors. I have been in meetings and conversations about the threat that gay marriage poses to the church and on and on and on.

The church is consumed with menial conversations that somehow feel important to them but confirm something truer for me. The church seems to be under the grip of fear—the fear of needing to be "saved" and the fear of doing something wrong and that "wrong thing" leading you to eternal damnation. Above all, I think the church is scared to lose their power. They have controlled the narrative for so long. They have been able to tell women and gay folks and people of color when and where they belong—and that power is seductive and laced with fear. I don't say all of this just to shit on the church. In fact, I love the church. I am still a pastor working to share the liberating message of Jesus with my community. The church is certainly not the only institution riddled with fear and power, but it is the one that gave me my own particular fear narrative that I have had to overcome. It might be the place that gave you yours too.

Or maybe your fear narrative came from our grossly obsessive diet culture and the fear that only one size of body is valuable and good. Maybe your fear narrative came from our patriarchal society in seeing men as the ultimate leaders and voices of authority. Honestly, even if you have never been to church, you have still encountered a pervasive and probably harmful narrative about what is "normal" or "good" or "valuable." When we buy into those false definitions of value and compare ourselves against them, we allow fear to grow and live. But do you know what has the power to dull out the sound of one really loud voice? Hundreds of voices together. Whether it is the institution of the church or the patriarchy or diet culture or your family or that one ex (we all have one)— whoever has the loudest, most powerful voice in your head— the only way to confront the lie is to speak truth and send a beam of light into that darkness and keep speaking until the whole thing breaks open.

11 FREEDOM IS ONLY REAL WHEN SHARED

When I was in middle school, back-to-school shopping was the big event of the year. Well, actually in middle school, any shopping is the big event of the year. Anyway, when we were growing up, my mom would almost exclusively take me and my sister shopping at Old Navy. Not only did Old Navy always have some sort of outrageous sale happening, but they were also one of the only stores in our neighborhood at the time that had black mannequins in the store and black models in their advertisements and in their commercials. You might be thinking that in the late '90s and early 2000s everyone had this sort of representation. They did not, and certainly not in suburban Colorado.

Here is what Old Navy knew: representation matters. It matters when people can see themselves in the story you're telling. For Old Navy it mattered for the purposes of selling clothes, specifically a lot of performance fleece in 1998. But for most of us, it matters so that that the freedom we find can be shared. After we came out, Sami and I *loved* taking pictures of each other and with each other. We loved it because it was something we didn't feel super confident doing when we were closeted, always wondering, *What if someone sees the pictures? Does this picture make it look like I love you? Is this too many pictures of just you to have in my phone?* And on and on and on. So when we came out and we could be as cute and obsessive as we wanted, we just loved taking pictures of our love. Also, probably an important side note: my wife is an incredible photographer, so good pictures are sort of her love language.

Now that we have found our freedom and have all these cute pics, we decided to really start sharing our love on Instagram. The beauty of social media is that you get to share whatever you want. I remember when we were in the closet, I would have given anything to see a lesbian couple on Instagram just living life and being happy and cute. It probably would have felt similar to how I felt seeing black mannequins in Old Navy. It would have felt like my story and my identity belonged in the world. Sometimes it is powerful just to see someone exist in a space that told them they shouldn't.

Fast forward many years later, and we are definitely still struggling on the black mannequin front, but on the other hand, LGBTQ representation has been steadily moving forward—especially on social media, where out and proud folks have not been holding back sharing who they are with the world. Nothing brings my heart more joy than to know that a young, closeted lesbian somewhere in Fort Myers, Florida, or Topeka, Kansas, can have an Instagram feed full of people being free. That representation can water the seed of what is possible in her mind. I would have given anything to see cute, happy lesbians on my Instagram feed, so now that I am here, I am happy to love my wife as publicly as possible.

I love the book and movie *Into the Wild*. Spoiler alert: I am about to tell you how it ends, but I don't even feel bad about it because it came out in 2007. If you haven't seen it by now, that's on you. It is a beautiful and inspiring story but also very sad. (There's the sticky truth again: sadness and beauty come from the same well.) The main character, Christopher, is looking for more meaning in life. He is tired of the hustle and materialism of his life, so he sets off for a solo adventure in the Alaskan wilderness. He has to figure out how to find his own food and keep himself safe and warm, and he chronicles everything he learns in a journal.

Toward the end of the book and his life (that's the spoiler), he has this one magnificent realization. The profound words he writes down in his journal are these: "Happiness is only real when shared."[2] He realized that he could have all of the happiness in the world up there in the Alaskan wilderness, but it wasn't real if he didn't get to share it. I believe the same is true with freedom. **Finding freedom only becomes real by the ways in which we share it and the ways in which we allow others to join us in it.**

One of the hardest things about being deep in the closet is that our love didn't feel real because it only existed inside the four walls we had built around ourselves. It was hidden and secret. I have never been so jealous of just seeing two people hold hands and walk down the street. That simple act felt like something I could never have. One day, very randomly, Sami reconnected with a friend of hers from college named Bonnie. They started talking and catching up, and it turns out that Bonnie was gay.

I cannot even tell you how happy Sami was to tell me this story. She was so excited to reconnect with her and talk to her. She finally felt like someone might actually understand what was happening. Bonnie lived near the beach, so one night we drove out there, and we had dinner and drinks while Sami caught up with Bonnie and I got to know her for the first time. It was wonderful and maybe the first time I had been in the

---

2. Jon Krakauer, *Into the Wild* (New York: Anchor, 1997), 189.

presence of someone who was so proudly talking about my same experience.

Do you remember the first moment you met someone or read someone's story about a situation that you felt like you were the only one going through? It is such a powerful moment and can be such a bright light at the end of the long tunnel. After dinner and drinks, Bonnie, Sami, and I walked down to the beach. It was pretty late at night, so the beach was empty and dark. Only the light of the moon was there, and we heard the sound of the waves crashing.

We talked more and shared more stories, and as we sat there in the sand, Bonnie looked at us and said, "You guys can like hold hands or something if you want. I know you're in love."

I know this sounds like a simple thing to say to two people, but it was honestly the most incredible feeling to truly be that seen and encouraged. We awkwardly laughed, and I grabbed Sami's hand. It was the first time we ever held hands outside of my room or my car, and it felt so magical.

Now that we are married and wake up next to each other every morning, sometimes I forget what it felt like when I thought I would never be able to hold her hand. I thought I would never be able to have one ounce of the life I have now. I didn't know any of this could be possible, but it took so many people like Bonnie, who stopped along the way and gave us those little moments of freedom. Some of those moments of freedom were given to us intentionally. Bonnie knew what it was like to be in the closet. She knew what it was like to have a secret relationship, and I think she knew what it would mean for us to hold hands on the beach that night. But there have also been moments where people have invited me into a newfound freedom and they didn't even know it.

When you are desperately looking for any signs of freedom, you start finding them everywhere. My wife wants a Tesla model X more than anything in life right now, and I swear, the more she talks about it, the more it feels like that is the only car on the road we ever see. I promise you if you start looking for freedom, you will find signs of it all around.

When I got my job as a pastor at a megachurch, I believed I had made it. Everyone around me reinforced my idea that I was the only one who ever thought about leaving, and not just leaving our church but leaving the whole idea of church altogether because it was ultimately pulling me away from the freedom I wanted. But I was so sure I was the only one. On one particularly quiet day at work, I ended up going to lunch with the woman in the office next to mine at the time named Joan. I am not sure that Joan and I had ever had a one-on-one conversation before this lunch date, but it was so great getting to know her better.

Very casually and confidently over lunch, she told me that she was thinking about leaving our church and her job. She said that she wanted to make a bigger impact, specifically in the area of homelessness and housing, and she thought that could be done more through another organization. Again, I know this sounds like such a simple statement, but I thought about this conversation for weeks! If Joan was thinking about leaving, who else dreamt of something different, and what did that mean for me? Could I leave too? It was another small reminder that there was life outside of the bubble I was living in. We find freedom when we are looking for it, and we find freedom when others share it. I know not everyone reading this book is in the closet and working at a church, but **whatever the thing is that feels like it is swallowing you whole, I promise there is freedom on the other side.**

When I see pictures of single mothers holding their babies while wearing their graduation cap and gown, I could cry. When people share about finally starting a family after a long and difficult journey of lost pregnancies and fertility treatment, I feel so grateful. Even my sister was the first black prom queen our high school had ever had, and I hope that made space for all the black and brown girls in suburban Colorado who wanted to do the same thing. **Each of us can use our stories to share the freedom that someone else might be desperately searching for.**

Nelson Mandela said it like this: "For to be free is not merely to cast off one's chains, but to live in a way that respects and enhances the freedom of others."[3] After our dinner with Bonnie, hearing her talk about girls she was dating and letting us hold hands and making it all feel so normal and good, I was on cloud nine. I finally understood what might be possible. Not long after that, I had my own opportunity to share that same freedom.

A few years before my world felt like it was being turned upside down, I met a young college student named Nicole. She was super smart and funny, and like all college students, she was full of infinite potential. I got the opportunity to become a mentor, friend, and just a general older person to talk to for Nicole and a few of her friends. But Nicole and I became close. After she had finished two years of college, she realized it was too expensive for her to continue, so she enlisted in the navy and went off for four years. She was stationed outside of Seattle, so she would come back to visit often. Every time she came back to visit, we would make time to catch up on life over a meal or a cup of coffee. When she was away, Sami and I would send her care packages and check on her often just to make sure she was doing all right.

On one of her visits home, while we were having coffee, Nicole, who is by no means comfortable with sharing (I always joke that I had coffee with her for two years before she told me

---

3. Mandela, *Long Walk to Freedom* (Boston: Back Bay Books, 1994), 624–25.

anything about her life), somehow mustered up the courage to tell me that she was gay. She shared that she was scared to tell me because she didn't know how I was going to respond. She knew I worked at a church that was nonaffirming.

My heart literally sank to the bottom of the chair. First and foremost, I told her how much I loved her and that I thought this was wonderful and beautiful and that it would not change a thing about our relationship. I asked her a bunch of questions and just felt so honored that she would share this part of herself with me. At the very same time, I felt like shit for not being as brave as she was being in this moment.

I left that coffee date and knew that I had to tell Nicole, and more than that, I wondered who else in my life might be watching me and waiting to find their own invitation to freedom. I couldn't believe how scared she was to tell me, and I just kept thinking, *If you only knew.* Have you ever had a secret or something you were scared to share and then someone opens up to you and shares the exact same thing?

The very next day, I was going to drive Nicole to the airport as she headed back to the navy base. I knew I had to tell her. Even though she was much younger than me, and she looked up to me as a mentor, I was so nervous to tell her this thing about me. In the car headed to the airport, I awkwardly stammered out, "Hey, remember what you told me at the coffee shop? Me too."

I told her about Sami and about wanting to leave my job but not knowing how. I apologized for keeping this secret in a way that made her unsure of whether she could come to me with her own truth. We had a moment in the car. I felt so relieved and so seen, and I hope she felt the same. At that point, Nicole and I had both only told a few people, and neither of us were sure what to do next.

My favorite part of this story is that just a few years later, after Nicole got out of the navy, finished undergrad, and started grad school, she is out and has a girlfriend she loves very much. She also lives in mine and Sami's back house! We have a whole lesbian compound that we have created. It warms my heart to see Nicole every day and be reminded of what it looks like to share freedom. Walking this journey together with Nicole is one of my favorite parts about our life in this house. The freedom we found in life doesn't come just so we can keep it to ourselves. The secrets we keep and the ways in which we hold back might actually be hurting more people than just ourselves. The prophet Brené Brown says that our healing is inextricably tied together, and I believe that with my whole heart. **Your freedom and healing and my freedom and healing need each other.** Whether you are the one looking for freedom or looking to share your freedom, we need you because **true freedom is only real when shared.**

12

HEALING FROM THE MOST UNEXPECTED PLACES

Church has been a part of my life for as long as I can remember. When I was in high school, my dad actually planted his own church, so our home became the hub for all things church. Rarely did even one day go by without some sort of church-related event—a midweek prayer meeting, Wednesday night Bible study, Thursday night choir rehearsal, and of course, Sunday service.

It was a lot, but I actually loved it. I was constantly around adults who loved me and genuinely cared about me. I was given opportunities and responsibilities that no other friends my age had. I gave the announcements every Sunday, and that is one of the experiences that I think has made me the communicator I am today and why I love speaking on stage so much.

Church did take up a good amount of our life, but for the most part, they were all good experiences. I decided to go to a Christian college because I loved church and what it could be and what it had meant to me to that point in my life. I was obviously aware of some of the larger issues happening in the church—misuse of money and misuse of scripture to oppress people (namely women and people of color), and of course, there were some people who seemed to take Christianity "too far." I didn't want to be associated with the worst of what the church could be, but I was okay with trying to figure out how to be a part of this thing called church and do my best to make it reflect what I thought it could be—a place for people to have community and connect with God. Simple, right?

Fast forward to being a woman of color who is also gay and the pastor at a church. Not only can it be hugely disappointing to see behind the curtain at a church but even more so to realize that behind the curtain people are having conversations about people like you. It was an awful place to be because at the same time as I was watching and experiencing the behind the scenes of the church, I was also deeply involved in the greater community of the church, and most of my friends (friends who felt like family) were a part of this church.

Sami didn't really start getting involved at church until she was in high school, but once she was in, she was all in. From high school youth group to Christian college to working at this church, Sami was deeply embedded in the church community. By the time we were ready to come out, our biggest question was, "What would life be like without church?"

We tried to guess which friends would still want to be a part of our lives, but we couldn't fathom that church would still be in our future. We had never seen an example of a gay Christian before. And when we came out, some of the things we feared most happened—and some of the most hurtful things that happened stemmed from the church. Some of our friends who felt like family didn't feel like family anymore. Some of our dearest friends who we asked to stand with us as bridesmaids at our wedding said no. They all had different reasons, but all the reasons had a common thread: their proximity to church. Whether it was what their church said about people like us or whether it was the church that they worked for threatening their position if they participated or even just not wanting to be judged by their own church community. They each had their reasons, and it did not feel good to be on the receiving end of those conversations. Beyond participation in our wedding, we had people who stopped talking to us. We got some nasty messages on the internet, and a few, very painful conversations were had. Do you know what every single one of these had in common? Church.

A few months after we came out, Sami and I were talking about how life without church almost felt naked. It felt good to be away from the toxic people and narratives, and we were still a bit shell shocked by the whole process. But we often wondered—would we ever go to church again? Would we ever have friends who felt like family again? It was a lonely and also beautiful season of digging and reaching the deepest parts of ourselves to find what we truly wanted. We were so very hurt by things that had been said and actions that had been taken. My goodness, some people's silence was deafening in this season, but in the midst of it all, I had a conversation with someone that changed the whole trajectory of our next season of life.

After I had posted the blog and everything was public, I got a random Facebook message from a guy named Cory. After some light internet stalking, I saw that Cory went to the same Christian college as me during the same years. We had a ton of mutual friends, and from what I could tell, Cory was a beacon of privilege. This tall, straight white guy with a wife and a few kids had just reached out to me out of nowhere and sent me this message: "Hey, Brittany, I've checked out your blog and your website. I appreciate your work and the way you speak honestly about your life. I'm interested in hearing more about your work with churches and curious about potential ways to collaborate. Let me know if you're available for a coffee to chat and so I can hear about the work you're doing with race, gender, sexuality, and inclusion."

I didn't even know what Cory did, and I definitely had no idea why this random white guy from my small Christian college wanted to talk to me about race, gender, sexuality, and inclusion. It felt weird, but honestly, at that point in my journey, I was in no place to pass up friends no matter how ambiguous the offer was.

Cory and I got coffee a few days later, and I found out that after our college years together, he also went on to become a pastor at a megachurch. He thought the trajectory of his life was set until he started asking bigger questions—questions about why certain people were not invited to the table. He started asking bigger questions about race and sexuality and money. He started questioning the very nature of church and its function. He told me his story about how asking these questions eventually led him out of his job. Even worse than that, I learned that asking these questions had caused him to be ostracized from his family. He had lost family, friends, and community from his decision to live a bigger story.

We talked and talked about what it felt like to have your whole identity tied to a place and then leave that place and not only leave, but not be welcomed back. We talked and talked, and then we got coffee again the next week and the next week. A few years have gone by, and we haven't gone a week without talking. Cory has become one of my best friends. Our stories, our lives, and even our personalities couldn't be more different, but the thing that binds us? We believe that the story was always meant to get bigger. We believe that everyone at any point has the capacity for transformation and healing—ourselves included. We believe that the story of God is so much more expansive than any of us understand, and we are very okay with pushing the boundaries and telling that story in a much larger way than we were told it. We don't believe there is some magical theology that, if you believe it right and say the right prayers, then your life will never be hard. Nope, being human is the hardest job any of us will ever have, and suffering is just a part of this life. But sometimes we get to decide what we suffer for. This life is going to be hard regardless, but choosing to go through some hard things is worth it.

I love Cory so much. He has taught me that you do not need to be gay to understand what it's like to make sacrifices and take losses to be who you are and believe what you believe. The experience of every gay Christian who comes out is unique, just like the experience of everyone like Cory is unique. But you know what ties them all together? The reality that we are all destined for change. We are destined for growth and evolution and stretching and pulling beyond what the people around you deem as normal. This process is so hard and definitely will cost you, but the alternative price is far too high to pay. The alternative is to not grow, not change, not evolve, and never become who you were meant to be. **It's**

going to be hard either way. Make sure you do the hard work that leads to your freedom.

It is not lost on me that, though most of my hurts came from church, that is also now the place where I get to stand on a stage and tell all of these stories to the most wonderful and fantastically strange group of people I have ever met. Cory and I get to be pastors together, and every single week, we tell our community that we believe in unity over uniformity. We don't want everyone to believe the same things or dress the same or live the same. We want everyone to be together and understand how healing true community can be.

I don't think it's an accident that so much of my healing has come from reclaiming the thing that hurt me. The same is probably true for you. **Our healing doesn't come from avoiding, pretending, or moving on. Our healing most times looks like going head-on into those wounds and reclaiming the things in our lives that we have lost.** Honestly, it also involves lots of therapy and being open to healing that comes from the most unlikely places. I have friends who are women and were told all their lives that women didn't have a place in leadership. They have found so much healing in raising daughters and telling them the opposite. I know so many people in the LGBTQ community who have lost parents through their coming-out experience, but they have older people who love them and can attempt to help fill the gaps. They have also become mentors to younger LGBTQ youth. I have friends who have gotten divorced and written guides for others who may be going through that same experience. There is a woman at our church who never had kids and now gets to become a mother to an entire community of millennials who are in desperate need of talking to someone with a little gray hair.

Life is hard—that is just factually true—but never buy into the lie that your pain or the hard things you went through are shameful or meant to be hidden. There is always something that can be reclaimed and used as a part of not only your healing but the healing of others. Wear it like a freaking badge of honor.

Several years ago, on my third year leading a civil rights tour through the South, we visited a museum in Jackson, Mississippi. Our guide was a beautiful black woman with dark skin, short hair, and an infectious smile. I was enjoying our time in the museum until we got to a new exhibit that was designed to take you on a journey from Africa to the auction block in the American South. Part of the exhibit involved walking through a life-sized slice of a slave ship. As you walk through it, you pass statues depicting how the bodies of the slaves would be stacked on one another and chained together. This portion of the exhibit was probably only ten feet long, but I couldn't even make it through the whole thing. Probably about four feet in I was so uncomfortable that I had to turn around, go around the exhibit, and meet the team on the other side.

Next our guide took us through the journey of arriving in America. She talked about how the slaves, already naked, would now be appraised and sold. Our museum guide was standing on what was meant to resemble an auction block. She held her fists together in front of her to resemble them being chained together. As she stood on that block, she recounted the whole journey and talked about all of the lives that had been lost along the way. She talked about lives that would be lost fighting in Africa. She talked about lives that would be lost getting to the ship. She talked about disease and hopelessness and trying to escape and all the lives that would be lost on the ships. She went on and on, and then she settled into where she was standing for a moment, looked down at her hands, and said, "Can you imagine?"

Before she finished the sentence in my head, I thought, *Yeah, can you imagine how much hate, how much shame, how much anger . . .* I was feeling so many variations of those three feelings in that moment, but this woman reframed all of it for me.

She looked down at her hands as she stood on this auction block and said, "Can you imagine the strength that it took to even get this far? That's the blood that runs in my veins, and that's why I'm a proud black woman."

I immediately began to weep. What happened in that moment was way more powerful than I could have ever imagined. This woman, through the story and narrative of what it means to be black in America, taught me how to be proud of who I am and what I've been through, not ashamed and not hateful. This woman gave me a sense to say, "Although that was massively painful, I'm still standing, I'm still here, and that says something about me. That says more about my strength than the people who hurt me, and I will not shrink my head down in shame. I will be proud of every single step I take moving forward because damn, it's been a long road."

I had never been prouder to be a black woman, and that pride came from reframing my understanding of one of the worst things that has happened to us. You would think that pride comes only from accomplishment and that healing comes from only good things, but here is what I actually think: **Our deepest journeys of healing happen when we are able to reclaim the very thing that hurt us, the very narrative that oppressed us, the very story that kept us small.**

I have been thinking a lot lately about my relationship to God and the church.

Once the church became the source (or at least I realized it had been the source) of pain and confusion, my natural response was to create as much distance as possible. Even though I went back to the church and reclaimed as much as I could and became a pastor again, I did so by detaching myself from the emotions of the church experience. The evangelical church has a long and successful history of manipulating emotions, including worship services led by professional musicians, perfectly timed lasers, and the exact right amount of fog at the exact right time. It's all meant to compel you to walk down to the front of the church and "give it all to God," even though you weren't even clear what you were giving. This happened to me more times than I can count. I now realize I was manipulated to think and act in a way that I not only was uncomfortable with but also didn't believe. Now, as I try to reclaim the narratives of my faith, I am finding that my approach to faith has become weirdly intellectual. In areas of my life where I have felt hurt or shame or manipulation, it is as if I am willing to experience healing only from a little bit of a distance.

I have read countless books on the black experience, the black power movement, and the civil rights movement. I intellectually understand the resilience and strength of my people, but standing in that museum that day, I let myself *feel*. And that was such an important moment.

With my faith, I have read so many books on deconstruction. I have done so much theological refraining and studying and understanding to be able to present the gospel not only in a way that I believe in but also in a way that I think might actually benefit the people around me. But I still experience a slight hesitation to really feel it. Sometimes even today I will be in church and my friends will be singing songs. I will begin to feel overcome with emotion and want to sing along or throw my hands up in the air, but I stop myself. Sometimes my life feels just overwhelming and I just want to cry out to God for help, but I stop myself. I stop myself because I feel like I haven't done enough intellectual work or because it feels too similar to the emotional manipulation of the past. I stop myself because . . . on and on and on.

Here's the thing—in the moments when I don't stop myself, when I actually let myself feel, I am amazed at what I find. I am in awe that something that feels so similar to the thing that hurt me now can bring such a depth of joy and peace.

Healing doesn't happen overnight, and it is not a one-time thing. This is a journey I get to be a part of every day. I get to reclaim what it means to be black and a woman. I get to reclaim what it means to be gay and a Christian every day. I get to remind myself that even if the mannequins in the store don't look like me, that is a reflection on a broken system, not a reflection of my value. I get to remind myself that even though there's still a giant pay gap between men and women, that is a reflection of a broken system and not a reflection of my value. Even though there are still many churches filled to the brim with people who think that me and my wife should not be together, that is a reflection of a misunderstanding of God and not a reflection on my value.

The people who have hurt me, the systems that have oppressed, and the churches that have manipulated me do not own me or you. They do not get to take away your joy, your healing, or your value. Don't think that you can't cry out to God and ask for help or feel proud of yourself. You get to do whatever you feel like doing. Being a human is freaking hard sometimes. Let yourself find healing, even if it feels strangely close to the thing that hurt you. There can be so much power in reclaiming that for yourself.

My hope for all of us is that as we go on these journeys of growing and evolving, make the people around us uncomfortable, confront small stories and harmful narratives, and find healing, and with every step of our journey, we can remember the strength we needed to even get this far. I hope the voice of our strength screams louder than any shame, fear, or regret in our heads. Listen, if you're reading this, it means you have made it this far. You have made it through every hard thing you have ever been through, and that says a lot about what you are capable of. So keep going.

My spiritual director once told me that fear lives in shallow breath, and I think they are right. I believe with my whole heart that one of the first things we can do to find freedom and our own healing is to not give fear a place to live. If you're looking for a place to start or are on a long road and looking for some fuel, or even if you just don't know what to do, let me offer you these simple words of wisdom as the great start to any new beginning. Breathe deeply. Fill your lungs with air, only to feel them empty again. Remind yourself that this is all a part of this thing called being human—deep breaths, fullness, and loss. Feel it all. Don't hold it in. **Don't let shallow breaths give room and board to your fear.** Breathe deeply, and go straight into the life that is calling to you, no matter what it costs.